# STAPLETON
## INTERNATIONAL AIRPORT

*To my family—the first was always for them.*

# STAPLETON
## INTERNATIONAL AIRPORT
*"The First Fifty Years"* by Jeff Miller

*Color photography by Pat Olson*

PRUETT **P** PUBLISHING COMPANY
Boulder, Colorado

First Edition
1 2 3 4 5 6 7 8 9

Printed in the United States of America

Library of Congress Cataloging in Publication Data

Miller, Jeffrey B., 1952-
    Stapleton International Airport: The First Fifty Years

    Bibliography: p.
    Includes index.
    1. Stapleton International Airport—History
I. Title
TL726.4.D58M54   1983      387.7'36'0978883      82-22975
ISBN 0-87108  614-X

# Acknowledgements

During the seven years it took me to research and write this book, many kind individuals gave their time and energy to what was little more than a dream. It would be impossible to list everyone by name—there were so many who helped—but certain people cannot go unmentioned, for without them this book would not have been written.

The actual idea for a history of Stapleton came from Jeff Davis. As a boy, he had fallen under the spell of flight while watching planes landing and taking off at Stapleton. Out of his childhood dreams came the idea for this book.

While I was doing research for the book, Robert Stapp, Stapleton's public affairs manager, became invaluable. He offered advice, gathered statistics and general information and arranged use of a helicopter for Pat Olson's aerial photographs. He was always ready to listen and help when I needed him—I cannot thank him enough.

A. D. Mastrogiuseppe, curator of photographs in the Western History Department of the Denver Public Library, also aided in the research of this book. "Augie" lent advice, assistance and an ear during the years of library work.

Two people who spent many hours with me reminiscing about the early days of aviation and Stapleton were Ray Wilson and Joseph Munshaw. Ray Wilson, who passed away a few years ago, was one of Colorado's aviation pioneers who helped form Monarch Airlines, which later became Frontier Airlines. Joe Munshaw, who worked for Continental Airlines for more than 20 years, filled in many details about the early days of Stapleton that I had not found in the library.

During the writing stage of this book I found two people in particular who made the final draft possible: Joe Nigg and Cathy Thomas. Joe Nigg tried to teach me how to use the English language properly, and Cathy Thomas spent many long and painful hours reading and rereading each chapter to catch my numerous mistakes.

I would also like to thank Robert Michael, director of the airport, and Mayor McNichols for granting me their valuable time for interviews.

And finally, I want to thank Betsy Friedman, Bob Thomas, Kathy Puckett and Pam Patrick for their help—with special thanks to Susan Burdick for her constant love, support and nimble fingers on a typewriter.

# Denver Mayors

| | | | |
|---|---|---|---|
| Benjamin Stapleton | 1923-1931 | Richard Batterton | 1959-1963 |
| George Begole | 1931-1935 | Thomas Currigan | 1963-1968 |
| Benjamin Stapleton | 1935-1947 | William McNichols | 1968-1983 |
| James Newton | 1947-1955 | Federico Pena | 1983 – |
| William Nicholson | 1955-1959 | | |

# Managers of Public Works
## (Previously Managers of Improvements and Parks)

| | | | |
|---|---|---|---|
| Charles Vail | 1927-1931 | William Shoemaker | 1960-1962 |
| W.B. Lowry | 1931-1935 | Walter Kstich | 1962-1963 |
| George Cranmer | 1935-1947 | William McNichols | 1963-1969 |
| T.P. Campbell | 1947-1955 | Richard Shannon | 1969-1972 |
| Richard Batterton | 1955-1959 | Harold Cook | 1972 – |
| Lester Cooley | 1959-1960 | | |

# Airport Managers

| | | | |
|---|---|---|---|
| W.F. Wunderlich | 1929-1930 | Charles Lowen | 1948-1951 |
| Irwin Lowry | 1931-1934 | David Davis | 1951-1959 |
| James Brownlow | 1935-1937 | Richard Martin | 1959-1963 |
| Charles Woodworth | 1937-1946 | Don Martin | 1963-1972 |
| John Curry | 1946-1948 | Robert Michael | 1972 – |

# Foreword

Stapleton International Airport is a testimonial to man's ability to look into the future—but not too far. Its history virtually parallels the history of commercial aviation; its future is as uncertain as next year's weather.

When the Denver Municipal Airport was opened in October 1929, it was variously described as "one of the most complete and safe aerial stations in the world"—and as a massive boondoggle. That difference of opinion has pretty well persisted throughout its existence. It probably will intensify as the argument rages over whether to expand it or abandon it.

But whatever the future holds, Stapleton's first fifty years has contributed to the high drama of man's conquest of the skies. The story of aviation is the story of the Wright brothers in their starched collars, tinkering at night in their bicycle shop in Dayton, Ohio; of barefoot youths gazing in awe at swaggering barnstormers in their leather jackets and octagonal goggles; of venturesome businessmen patching together a dozen rickety airlines into a transcontinental carrier.

Likewise, the story of Stapleton Airport is the story of the men and events that transformed a 640-acre patch of sandy prairie into one of the ten busiest airports in the world. Unlike most of the major hub airports in the United States, the terminal still stands on the same ground it occupied fifty years ago. That lends a continuity to its history that is rare in the fast-changing world of flight.

It is perhaps now safe to say that the judgment of the city officials who authorized an expenditure of $143,013.37 to buy those 640 acres of sagebrush has been vindicated—although the decision was hotly disputed at the time. Had they had the foresight to buy 15,000 acres, they might have averted the wrangling that is going on fifty years later.

The changes that were wrought in those fifty years are chronicled in this book by a young Denver man, Jeff Miller, who has a fascination with the past and a feel for living history. He has captured much of the color and the controversy that has swirled around this aerial crossroads of the Rocky Mountain West since its inception.

For those interested in airports, *Stapleton International Airport: The First Fifty Years* will be absorbing reading. For those interested in the people who built a remarkable institution, it will be a vital link between yesterday and tomorrow.

ROBERT STAPP
PUBLIC AFFAIRS MANAGER, 1971—1982
STAPLETON INTERNATIONAL AIRPORT

# Table of Contents

*In the early days of aviation, air shows traveled the country thrilling crowds. More importantly, these aerial circuses helped promote aviation and prepare people for the coming age of air transportation. Courtesy of the Western History Department, Denver Public Library.*

# Prologue

With the historic flight of the Wright brothers' biplane at Kitty Hawk, North Carolina, on December 17, 1903, mechanized flight became a reality to the American people. But experiments in air travel had been taking place around the world for generations. Man's desire to soar with the birds had led to hand-held wings, man-sized kites and hot air balloons long before the invention of the internal combustion engine gave him the idea of mechanized air travel.

In the early 1900s the airplane, or "aeroplane," had no practical purpose. Those who wanted to build and fly these new inventions had to find a way to make money from them to support themselves. Many of the early flyers, like the Wright brothers and Glenn H. Curtiss (who developed the Curtiss model biplanes and later the Curtiss monoplanes), formed exhibition companies which toured the country promoting aviation and raising money to develop and build better aircraft. These men and their traveling airshows were the precursors of the "barn-storming" pilots that crisscrossed the country staging aerial shows after World War I.

## The Federal Government Learns To Fly

In the early 1900s, the federal government could not ignore the extensive newspaper coverage of developments in aviation. Militarily, the government began to experiment with the idea of using the new airplane as a battle spotter—rather than war balloons—and with the future possibility of utilizing the plane in actual combat. On August 7, 1907, the aeronautical division of the U.S. Army Signal Corps was formed to investigate these possibilities. This division was called the Army Aviation Service (renamed the U.S. Army Air Corps on July 2, 1926) and was staffed by one officer and two enlisted men. More than a year passed before the Army Aviation Service performed its first mission in its own plane.

When World War I broke out in 1914, the Army's air service had grown to 55 planes and 65 officers, 35 of whom were fliers. The war in Europe had devastating results for both people and industry, but for aviation it was a catalyst that brought about increased aircraft development and acceptance.

While the military uses of the airplane were being studied by the federal government in the early 1900s, the commercial uses of the plane were also being explored. The airplane was still too unreliable for flying passengers on a commercial basis, but mail was a different matter. Congress passed the first "Air Mail" bill in 1910, which appropriated funds to determine the feasibility of scheduling regular airmail flights from one city to another. No full-scale operation was immediately launched, due in part to World War I. After the war, however, the commercial possibilities were reexplored.

## Airmail Service Begins

After World War I, the Army Aviation Service developed a plan for flying the mail between Washington, D.C., Philadelphia and New York City. On May 15, 1918, the Service began a three-month test period of the route. The experiment was deemed a success and Congress appropriated more funds to establish a transcontinental airmail route.

At this point, the U.S. Post Office assumed responsibility from the Army for carrying the mail and began to buy planes and hire pilots. In July 1919, the Post Office began flying the first leg of a transcontinental route, New York City to Chicago. By September 1920, the service was extended to San Francisco, completing the first crosscountry airmail route, called the "Columbia" route. On February 2, 1921, postal flyers inaugurated night flying of the mail. Because few airports were properly lit for night flying, the pilots were supplied with flashlights and railroad maps for navigation, and farmers were organized along the route to light bonfires as guiding beacons.

## Private Enterprise Begins Flying The Mail

In February 1925, Congress passed the Kelly Act, a plan to see if private airline companies could fly the mail more efficiently and safely than the Post Office. The first phase of the Act was to offer private contractors the airmail "feeder" routes, which linked the Columbia route to population centers not on the direct route. On

July 15, 1925, the postmaster general advertised for bids on these feeder routes. By 1926, private contractors were flying the mail and a limited number of passengers along the feeder routes while the Post Office continued to operate the Columbia route. The transcontinental route, however, remained under the control and operation of the Post Office until 1927, when it was transferred to private airlines.

During this time, the crash of the dirigible, *Shenandoah,* and the criticism of aviation by Billy Mitchell, the WWI flying ace, forced President Coolidge to form the Morrow Board. The purpose of the board was to study aviation and what role the government should play in its regulation. The board's recommendations resulted in the Air Commerce Act of 1926. This Act separated civilian and military aviation, placing civilian aviation under the control of the Department of Commerce and military aviation under the responsibility of the armed services.

## Lindbergh Advances the Cause of Aviation

Nineteen hundred twenty-seven was by far the most important year for the future of aviation, and all because of the act of one man: Charles A. Lindbergh. On May 20, 1927, the ex-airmail pilot from St. Louis took off for France and destiny. This single courageous act captured the imagination of the whole world when, 33 and a half hours later, Lindbergh landed in Paris. No other single act helped aviation more than this historic flight, for it caught the world's attention and gave Lindbergh—by then a world hero—an audience to whom he could promote aviation.

## Technological Advances

While aviation was making headway in the eyes of the public, developments in aircraft and technological equipment were making airplanes and their operation safer. By the late 1920s, the single-engine, open-cockpit biplane was being pushed aside by sealed-cabin, mono-wing planes with as many as three engines. Wood and canvas construction had been superceded by all metal planes (like the Ford 4-AT tri-motor), that could carry as many as 32 passengers (like the Fokker F-32).

In 1928, weather information began to be transmitted by teletype. In 1929, James Doolittle developed a system that made it possible to make the first successful instrument landing. The variable-pitch propeller was developed, which allowed an aircraft's propeller blades to vary their pitch and setting into the airflow to suit the different demands of take-off and high-speed flight.

Also during the 1920s, the two-way radio was developed by two men, Thorp Hiscock and Herbert Hoover, Jr. (son of President Hoover). They pooled their research and, by 1930, had perfected the two-way radio for planes. (Western Air Express, in conjunction with Boeing Air Transport, was first to use an early version of the two-way radios on November 6, 1928.)

## Airports: The Natural Result of Aviation

As man tinkered and refined the new airplane, developing a whole new mode of transportation, the need for airports quickly became apparent. In the early days of aviation, though, all a plane needed to take off and land was a level field, track or road. If there was a barn nearby it could serve as a storage shed or makeshift repair shop. With a fuel truck or the installation of a small gas pump in front of the barn, an airport could suddenly be born.

These haphazard airports were able to handle the limited number of planes flying in the early 1900s, but as aviation enthusiasm grew and the number and type of aircraft increased, these airports were pushed to their limits. Newly developed airplanes with bigger payloads and increased horsepower demanded greater runway lengths, larger hangars and more sophisticated repair shops. For an airport to remain functional—and thereby profitable—in this time of aviation growth, it had to constantly expand and alter its service.

But airplanes were not the only problem facing the early airports. As people began flying as passengers, airports began to serve two masters: aircraft and passengers. By the late 1920s, a successful airport was one that catered to the comfort of passengers almost as much as to the airline companies and pilots.

These problems did not, however, deter many from entering the airport business, for by 1928, 25 years after the Kitty Hawk flight, there were approximately 1,000 airports across the country. They ranged from the barn/field/pump variety to those utilizing paved runways, air terminals, machine shops and hangars. In the years to come, with the rapid development of aircraft and increasing numbers of passengers, many of these airports would die or become backwater facilities.

The airports that did survive the evolution of aviation and grow into major facilities are worth studying, for they are as much a part of aviation history as the airplane itself. The history of airports and aviation have become so intertwined that to study one brings into focus the history of the other. Stapleton International is one such surviving airport. Starting from 640 acres of dairy-farm land, Stapleton has grown to nearly 10 times that size and is currently the eighth busiest airport in the world.

But that kind of growth, taking place over Stapleton's 50-year history, did not happen by itself. Many

*In 1925 the Kelly Act was passed by Congress. This gave the job of flying the mail to private contractors, a job previously handled by the Post Office. One of the early biplanes used was the Boeing model 95 (1929). Courtesy of Western Airlines.*

politicians, community leaders, military personnel and general citizens—acting both as supporters and opponents of the airport—comprise the real history of Stapleton International Airport. Through their attempts at forecasting the future, they took risks, made mistakes and fought with determination for their point of view. Thus, to study the history of Stapleton is to discover the history of Denver and its people.

*This Boeing model 40-B-4 (1930) was also used to fly mail. In addition to the mail, these early planes carried passengers brave enough to weather an open cockpit. The passenger was issued goggles, leather cap, parachute (sometimes), and had to sit with mail sacks at his feet. Courtesy of Western Airlines.*

*The first recorded engine-powered flight in Colorado. Louis Paulhan, a French aviator, put on a three-day exhibition at Overland Park on February 1-3, 1910. Courtesy of the Colorado Aviation Historical Society.*

# Chapter One

The Denver Municipal Airport was conceived
at another crisis in this city's oldest
problem—maintenance of its position on the
main lines of transportation.

This statement was made in the official dedication program issued at the opening of Denver's municipal airport, October 17–20, 1929. Called the "Union Station of the Air," and heralded as the most modern facility in the country, the Denver Municipal Airport was constructed by the city in an effort to attract a new and vital means of transportation. Many saw the building of the airport as a way of insuring Denver's future growth and prosperity.

During Denver's more than 100-year history, the city has had to continually face major transportation crises that have threatened its very existence, and all from the same source: the Colorado Rocky Mountains. This natural landmass, covering almost two-thirds of the highest state in the Union, has been the blessing/curse of Denver since the city's founding along the banks of the Cherry Creek in the 1850s. Without the mountains' wealth of wildlife, timber and minerals, Denver might never have developed, for the city began as a supply center for those tapping the natural resources of the mountains.

But the Rockies, while offering so much, also deterred all means of transportation to and from the West. The early West Coast "bull trains" carrying provisions to Denver had to first travel north or south to traverse the less rugged mountains of Wyoming or New Mexico before entering Colorado and heading for Denver. In spite of the longer routes, the wagons kept coming because of the city's importance as a regional supply center. No matter how long it took West Coast supplies to reach Denver there were enough people in the area to make the trip profitable. However, with the beginning of construction of the transcontinental railroad, the continuation of supplies to Denver was threatened.

## Denver's First Transportation Crisis

Although Denver would have been a natural stop in any transcontinental railroad system because of its growing population and regional importance, the railroads had to bypass the city because of the Rocky Mountains. It was felt the Colorado mountain range was impenetrable. Instead, Cheyenne was chosen as a stop on the cross-country route because Wyoming's

mountains were less rugged. On May 10, 1869, the Union Pacific and Central Pacific railroads joined in Promontory, Utah, completing the route.

Many of Denver's leading businessmen and local politicians realized the implications of not being part of this route—Denver's future growth and prosperity were at stake. Led by such men as David H. Moffitt and John Evans, they banded together and had a branch, or "spur" line, built between Denver and Cheyenne. Later, Denver's citizens built spur lines south and east to link up with other major rail lines. Only through Denver's initiative did the city connect with this important transportation system and solve its first major transportation crisis.

## Denver's Early Aviation

With the advent of the airplane, the Colorado Rockies once again posed a problem for a new means of transportation. Many early aviators thought planes could not fly over Colorado's mountains, let alone handle Denver's high altitude.

In an effort to dispel these feelings and promote aviation in Colorado, the *Denver Post*, in the summer of 1909, offered prizes totaling $10,000 for the first demonstration of a mechanically propelled flight in Colorado. The contest had a six-month time limit. Further, any plane that entered had to carry a passenger and fuel for a trip of no less than 125 miles and be able to reach a speed of at least 40 miles per hour. Eight airplane builders officially entered the contest, six of whom were from Colorado, but no recorded demonstration ever took place during the six-month period.

The first recorded engine-powered flight in Colorado occurred February 1, 1910, just over a month after the *Denver Post's* contest deadline had passed. Louis Paulhan, the French "birdman," who traveled the country staging flying exhibitions, was contracted by F. B. Hutchinson, a Denver businessman, to fly in Denver. Paulhan arrived in Denver accompanied by his wife, 35 mechanics, engineers and workmen, and his Farman biplane.

Paulhan's publicity man had arrived in Denver a few days before to promote the event. The exhibition

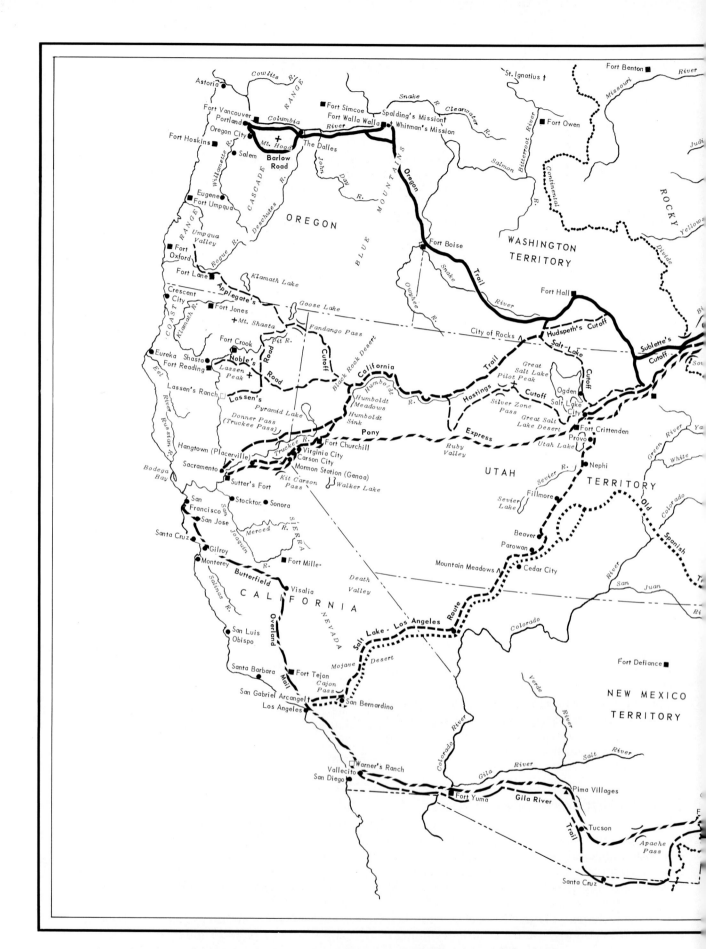

*The Rocky Mountains formed a great land barrier that effectively isolated Denver from direct routes to the West Coast. Major trails established during the mid- to late 1800s, therefore, ran either north or south of Denver to traverse*

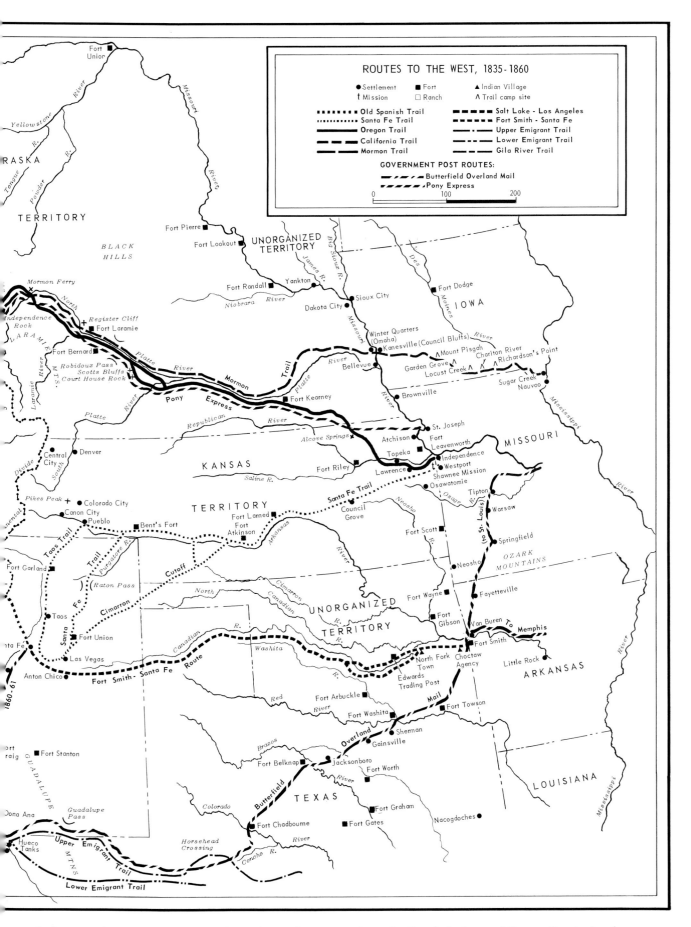

*the less rugged mountains. Following the Civil War, the transcontinental railroad also bypassed Denver, threatening the city's potential as a major transportation center. Courtesy of Western History Department, Denver Public Library.*

needed little promoting, for Paulhan had made national news a few days before when he had broken a previous altitude record by soaring to a height of 5,000 feet in an aerial show in Los Angeles. By the time the French aviator arrived in Denver, everyone in the surrounding area had heard of his feat and wanted to see him do it again.

The city aided this momentous event by running a special train and tramcars from Denver to Overland Park, where the pilot was scheduled to put on a three-day exhibition. Overland Park, a 30-acre area along the Platte River just west of Broadway, was a racetrack that had level ground, which made it a perfect runway for Paulhan and his plane. The city also took down some high fences that could have gotten in the plane's way and sent a dozen policemen—six on horseback—to control any crowds.

Everyone, especially the policemen, were surprised when the biggest crowd in Denver's history, 40,000 to 50,000 people, assembled in the early afternoon of February 1 to see Paulhan's scheduled three o'clock flight. On his first attempt, the plane rose 20-30 feet off the ground for only a matter of seconds. F. P. Gallagher, a *Rocky Mountain News* reporter, wrote on February 2, 1910:

> Before the biplane mounted into the air, the thousands of spectators in the park and on the surrounding hills speculated with something like awe as to what sort of sorcery they were about to behold, and after the queer device of wood and canvas had swept out into the field, jumped into the air and fluttered like a barnyard fowl for a few seconds, they looked at one another, as if to inquire, "is this the miracle we came out to see."

More than half of the disappointed audience left after the second attempt. But on the third attempt, Paulhan made it aloft. With a shudder and a roar he and his plane were off, rising to an estimated 100-300 feet (an accurate measurement of his altitude was difficult because of the fading light). Making his first turn of the day, Paulhan headed back toward the field hoping to land, only to find the remaining crowd of more than 10,000 had trampled down the fences and swarmed over the field. Paulhan buzzed the crowd once, then made another turn before finding a stretch of open field where he landed.

On the third day of the exhibition, just when he had coaxed the plane 20 feet off the ground, the plane began "acting up" and Paulhan crash landed into a group of spectators. Three people had minor injuries, Paulhan was unhurt. His plane, however, was totally destroyed. The engine continued running after the crash, digging a hole in the ground with the propeller. Paulhan had to jump out of the cockpit and turn off the motor by hand.

Just after the incident (the first recorded airplane crash in Colorado), Paulhan discovered most of his plane had been stolen by souvenir-seeking people.

## Aviation Gains Ground in Denver

The year 1910 also witnessed the founding of many Denver aviation companies. The General Aviation Company began manufacturing planes to operate and sell. The market being somewhat limited, the company had to put on aerial exhibitions to earn money. Also started in 1910 was the Mattewson Aeroplane Company. E. Linn Mattewson and Walter Marr formed this company and had their offices on Court Place, between Sixteenth and Seventeenth streets. On July 21, 1910, they flew their first plane at an "aerodome" on Monaco Boulevard, one mile east of City Park. The plane rose 20 feet and traveled 100 feet. After the company's only pilot was killed in an air accident in 1913, the company dropped out of the airplane business and entered the automobile industry.

In the early 1900s, airplanes were such a fascination to people that any place a plane was, a crowd was sure to gather. Because of this fact, the Colorado State Fair Committee decided to hold an air exhibition during its 1910 fair. The exhibition took place in Pueblo at the state fair grounds on September 3. A group of flyers and airplanes assembled but not one was able to get off the ground.

After the state fair aerial fiasco, three Colorado aviators, Walter Brookins, Arch Hoxsey and Ralph Johnstone, decided to put on their own exhibition at Overland Park, November 17–20, 1910. The first day 25,000 people came to watch and all three planes rose off the ground. Hoxsey flew to a height of 3,500 feet, showing that Colorado's altitude was no deterrent to flying, while Brookins and Johnstone gave an exhibition of "skillful flying." Unfortunately, Johnstone was killed that day when his plane stalled and dove to the ground.

Jack Payment and Art Wagner (later responsible for the Denver-built Wagner biplane) were two more Colorado aviators experimenting with the airplane. On one attempt at flight in 1910 they crash-landed into Berkeley Lake. This gave them the novel idea of attaching pontoons onto the wheels of the plane. Within a year they had made Denver's first amphibian aircraft and demonstrated it on Sloan's Lake.

The first record of a Denver-built plane being flown in Colorado was on August 4, 1911; the pilot was George W. Thompson. The *Rocky Mountain News* reported that George Thompson was not his real name, but his assumed aviator's name. The pseudonym was used because Thompson had an "aged" mother who, if she knew what her son was doing, would "collapse under the strain." Thompson gave a three-day exhibition, flying his Mattewson biplane from the Jefferson County fairgrounds at Lakeside.

Within a few years, airplanes became more stable and reliable. The first Colorado passenger taken aloft—other than an aviator—was H. V. Deuell, a *Rocky Mountain News* reporter. (The *Denver Post*, not wanting to be outdone, sent Ralph Baird, a *Post* photographer, up in an airplane a short time later.) Deuell flew in a Denver-built Wagner biplane on February 28, 1914, from the hangar at Manhattan Beach, an amusement park on the north shore of Sloan's Lake. (This park had been built in 1890 and called the Sloan's Lake Resort. After a fire, it was rebuilt in 1891 and renamed Manhattan Beach. The park lasted until 1914, when the competition from Elitch Gardens became too tough.) The plane rose 30 feet into the air and traveled 16 miles in 15 minutes. Deuell's impression of flying as stated in the *Rocky Mountain News*, March 1, 1914, was: "The sensation, I imagine, could be duplicated by riding a rocking chair on a cloud, there was no sense of insecurity. Thought of danger from wind and height was lost in the intoxication of the most wonderful excitement man has succeeded in inventing for his amusement."

## Denver's Second Transportation Crisis

By 1918, the federal government realized the airplane's potential as an airmail carrier and decided to develop a transcontinental airmail route. When the route (called the Columbia route) was mapped out by the Post Office, Denver was bypassed as it had been by the railroads earlier. Once again, Cheyenne was picked as a stopover rather than Denver. The Post Office's reason for this was the same as the railroad's reason in the 1860s: the Rocky Mountains. The early biplanes had difficulty obtaining the altitude necessary to climb over the Colorado Rockies, so it was felt flying over the mountains outside of Cheyenne would be safer.

When the Kelly Act was passed by Congress in February 1925 (a plan to transfer airmail service from the Post Office to private enterprise), the postmaster general was authorized to take bids from private operators on the transcontinental's "feeder" routes. These feeder routes linked the Columbia route with cities not on the main transcontinental route. If a contractor did not bid on the feeder route from Cheyenne to Denver, the city would once again be facing a transportation crisis. But the feeder route of Cheyenne-Denver-Pueblo being offered through the Kelly Act, appeared much too lucrative to ignore.

The lucrative nature of the route came directly from Denver's growing regional importance. Colorado Airways, founded by Anthony F. Joseph, guaranteed

Denver's connection to the Columbia route when the company bid on and was awarded the Cheyenne-Denver-Pueblo airmail route. On May 31, 1926, Colorado Airways began flying the route and, thus, linked Denver for the first time with the transcontinental air route. Denver's second transportation crisis was over, with Denver having done nothing to solve it. (On December 10, 1927, after Colorado Airways experienced financial difficulties, Western Air Express took over the route.)

## A Different Type of Transportation Crisis Arises

By late 1926/early 1927, Denver businessmen and politicians were beginning to see the increasing importance of the airplane as a means of transportation for passengers as well as goods. If Denver was to efficiently and effectively become a part of the country's rapidly growing and expanding aviation industry, it would have to plan ahead.

Independent airline companies and airfields had been forming in Denver since the early 1920s, but with no cohesiveness: In 1922 it was announced that plans were being made to establish a commercial airplane factory at Humphrey's Field, located at Twenty-sixth and Oneida. In 1925, Alexander Industries, located at what later became Englewood Field, began manufacturing the Eaglerock airplane, which was one of the first mass-produced planes and led the field in aircraft sales in 1927. Curtiss Wright Field (which changed its name to Park Hill Field, later to Haydeon Air Field, and still later to Vest Field) was one of the earliest airfields in the Denver area. Combs Airpark, originally called Lowry Airport, began operating in 1924. Englewood Airport opened in 1925. The Adams City Airport was established in 1927 and renamed "Lindbergh Field" after the aviator made his world-famous flight to Paris.

Many of Denver's businessmen and politicians saw this uncontrolled and random growth of aviation as an ultimate threat to Denver's aviation standing across the country. If Denver wanted to be in the forefront of this rapidly developing industry, the city had to somehow consolidate the local aviation community.

## Plans for a Municipal Airport Are Born

One way of achieving this goal of consolidation was through the construction of a municipal airport. The leader of the fight to build such an airport was Benjamin F. Stapleton. Stapleton was mayor of Denver from 1923–1947, with the exception of the 1931–1935 term, and led the city through many major problems and

GEORGE THOMPSON READY FOR
FLIGHT IN MATHEWSON FLYER
MATHEWSON AEROPLANE CO.
DENVER, COLO.

*George Thompson (his aviator's name) was one of
Colorado's early home-grown flyers. Courtesy of the
Colorado Aviation Historical Society.*

Deuell Is First
-Professional to
Fly in State.

*The first passenger taken aloft in Colorado (other than an
aviator) was Harvey V. Deuell, right, Rocky Mountain
News reporter, on February 28, 1914. His pilot was Chris J.
Petersen. Excerpted from the* Rocky Mountain News,
*courtesy of the Colorado Historical Society.*

10

The first airplane repair shop in Denver, called the Tavern Garage and Airplane Repair Depot, was located at 2955 Larimer St. It was open from 1919 to 1920 and owned by F.A. Van Dersarl. Courtesy of the F.A. Van Dersarl collection, Colorado Aviation Historical Society.

In 1929 Luella Perkable (Perky) became the first woman in Colorado to parachute from a plane. Jumping from an altitude of 2,100 feet, she was forced to draw her chute from a cannister attached to the side of the ship. Jack Euler was her pilot. Courtesy of the Colorado Aviation Historical Society.

*Denver Union Airport, a privately owned airport near Vest Field, was representative of the numerous small airports serving the Denver area in the 1920s. Courtesy of the Western History Department, Denver Public Library.*

*One of the first mass-produced airplanes in the country was the Eaglerock, manufactured by Alexander Industries of Denver. This is the first Eaglerock, which had a Curtiss OX-5 engine of 90 h.p. and was first flown in 1925. Courtesy of the Western History Department, Denver Public Library.*

The structural design and construction of an early airplane can be seen in this construction of a Grey Goose Airline plane. Grey Goose was one of many small companies that sprang up in Denver during the early days of aviation. Courtesy of the Western History Department, Denver Public Library.

crises in its growth and development. Although Stapleton is known more for his promotion and protection of agricultural interests, in the case of the municipal airport Stapleton stood firm and resolute. The city of Denver, he believed, needed a point of consolidation for its growing aviation industry, and a municipal airport would be the answer.

It has been reported that Stapleton began thinking of a municipal airport as soon as he took office in 1923. He and his commissioner of parks and improvements, Charles D. Vail, believed it was paramount to the future of Denver's national aviation standing that a plan of consolidation be implemented. (The commissioner of parks and improvements was a part of the early planning because Mayor Stapleton thought a municipal airport would legally fall under that department). The city, these two politicians knew, could not dictate to private enterprise what should be done to consolidate aviation, but they felt a municipal airport—owned and operated by the city, and offering the most modern equipment and services available—would naturally draw the major

airline companies and pilots to it. This would indirectly unify Denver's aviation industry and give it a focal point from which future growth and development would come. After Stapleton and Vail had discussed the idea, Stapleton sent Vail on a tour of the country to review other airfields, talk to aviators and executives of airline companies and seek advice from the Department of Commerce in Washington. Vail first traveled through the Southwest, then attended the meeting of the Aeronautical Chamber of Commerce in Cleveland. From there, he continued to the East where he visited airfields and talked to representatives of the Department of Commerce.

In the early planning stages of the airport, many possible sites were suggested. One of these was the Sand Creek site, approximately six miles from the center of Denver. The Sand Creek, sometimes called "the Sand Dunes," or "Rattlesnake Hollow," was east of Colorado Women's College and northwest of Fitzsimmons General Hospital. The center of the proposed tract of rolling, sandy hills was at East Thirty-second Avenue and Wabash Street.

*Lowry Airfield (later named Combs Air Park) was another privately-owned field in the Denver area. Its borders were Holly St., 38th Avenue, Dahlia St. and the Union Pacific railroad tracks. Courtesy of the Western History Department, Denver Public Library.*

Stapleton and Vail favored this site because of its location away from any developed area and because land prices there were less than those closer to downtown Denver. A large tract of the site was owned by the Holstein Land Company of which H. Brown Cannon, a personal friend of the mayor's, was a major shareholder. The land was used by the Windsor Farm Dairy as a dairy farm. Another parcel of the site was owned by the estate of Samuel Hertsel, who had died November 20, 1918.

It is interesting to note that H. Brown Cannon also owned the option on the Hertsel property and stood to profit substantially from the city buying both parcels of land. Many Denver citizens believed the site was backed by Stapleton specifically because Cannon owned the land. Although this might have been true, no illegality on Cannon or Stapleton's part was ever proved.

Another proposed plan for the airport suggested the airfield could be constructed so it adjoined Lowry Air Field (later known as Combs Airpark) which was bounded by East Thirty-eighth Street, Dahlia Street, Holly Street and Smith Road. Using this site, the plan's

proponents argued, expenses could be shared with the state; Lowry housed the 120th National Guard Squadron which was financed by the state. Charles Lindbergh, when he stopped in Denver on a national tour sponsored by the Guggenheim Fund to promote aviation, also said that he believed this plan to be a good way of deferring expenses.

To decide the issue, the Denver City Council formed committees to review the different sites and talk with aviation experts. By this time, however, Stapleton had decided he wanted the Sand Creek site and began applying pressure to the City Council. In December 1927, he took some of the members to the Sand Creek site: they included Thomas F. Dolan, president of the council; Louis Straub, Arthur Weiss and Harry Chrysler, members of the council's aviation committee; and Frank Dodge, postmaster. In "freezing temperatures," Stapleton dug up shovelfuls of dirt to show the others the ground could support an airport. (Opponents of the Sand Creek site believed the site's soil was too sandy and porous to properly support runways).

*The 1929 Eaglerock Bullet, the most popular of Alexander's planes, supposedly could carry "four people and a dog" at nearly 130 m.p.h. It sold for $6,666. Courtesy of the Western History Department, Denver Public Library.*

## Opposition to the Airport Forms

On December 13, 1927, the *Rocky Mountain News* reported that aviators connected with the city's committees working on the airport problem were virtually unanimous in opposing the Sand Creek site. Two important opponents were Major Bruce Kistler, commander of the 120th Observation Squadron of the National Guard stationed at Lowry Air Field, and city councilman, George P. Steele. Kistler opposed the site because of its sandy soil and distance from Denver's downtown. He was in favor of having the field adjoin Lowry. Steele opposed not only the site, but the very concept of having the city spend taxpayers' money to finance and operate a municipal airport.

On March 19, 1928, the city council passed an ordinance that approved the purchase of the Sand Creek site. It did not, however, appropriate the necessary funds. The appropriation meeting was scheduled six days later, March 25. The council had heard the report of a Lieutenant Lyman S. Peck, an engineer who had been

*Benjamin F. Stapleton, for whom the airport is named, was mayor of Denver from 1923-1947 (with the exception of the 1931-1935 term). It was through his perseverance that Denver built a municipal airport and, therefore, assured itself of an important place in aviation's future. Courtesy of the Western History Department, Denver Public Library.*

*In 1927 Mayor Ben Stapleton and other members of the municipal airport commission debated a number of possible sites for the new airport. The Clayton College site and the East 38th Avenue site were heavily favored by local aviation experts, who believed those sites had better soil characteristics than the Sand Creek site, favored by the mayor. Stapleton contended that his choice would save the city money because of the site's low purchase price. His critics countered that the Sand Creek site was too far from the central business district to serve as an airport. The distance from downtown Denver to the Sand Creek site was seven miles. Excerpt from the Rocky Mountain News, courtesy of the Colorado Historical Society.*

## WHICH SITE WILL BECOME CITY AIRPORT?

A VIATION experts of the city have failed to agree with certain members of the municipal airport committee led by Mayor Stapleton on the best location for the city's municipal flying field. Experienced fliers of the city are said to favor the Clayton College or E. 38th ave. sites, while the mayor is said to favor the Windsor Farm Dairy site. Aviation leaders object to the mayor's choice on the grounds that the contour and location of the land is not suitable for a flying field, while the mayor declares the sites chosen by the other men are too expensive. Aviation leaders have declared repeatedly that the Windsor Farm Dairy site is much too far from the business district of the city to be of any real value as an airport. The mayor is also said to be giving some consideration to the E. 48th ave. site.

*Charles D. Vail, Denver manager of Improvements and Parks, was Stapleton's right-hand man in the purchase and building of Denver Municipal Airport. Courtesy of the Western History Department, Denver Public Library.*

*These plans were prepared by Lyman S. Peck, city engineer, and presented to Mayor Stapleton as to the airport's layout if the Sand Creek site was chosen. Excerpt from the* Rocky Mountain News, *courtesy of the Colorado Historical Society.*

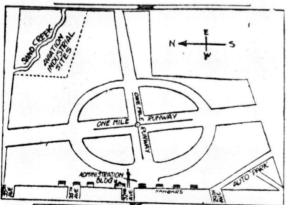

HERE is the way Denver's municipal airport will look, if laid out according to the plans of Lyman S. Peck, engineer, at the Sand Creek site favored by Peck, Mayor Stapleton and the city council. The sketch was taken from plans drawn by Peck and presented to Mayor Stapleton.

retained by Stapleton to report on the proposed airport sites. The report gave the Sand Creek site the highest marks in comparison with other sites being discussed. Peck was also retained by the city to draw up plans for the new airport—see sketch below—but the plans were later abandoned and others adopted.

Steele, the major opponent of any municipal airport, was absent, for unknown reasons, from the ordinance meeting on March 19. Finding he had not had his say, Steele began complaining loudly to the newspapers. His objections carried considerable weight, for he was a widely known attorney and candidate for the Colorado Supreme Court. Steele announced, on March 22, that the city had no authority to purchase a municipal airport, and the whole airport "scheme" was without legal foundation. He continued in a *Denver Post* article of March 20, 1928: "The city has no more right to enter the airport business than it would have to build and operate a union station for railroad trains or motor buses. Clearly, the establishment of an airport is a commercial venture, and as such is outside the city's powers."

The journalist who wrote the article, obviously, agreed with Steele, for he editorialized (although not stated as such) by writing: "Against the wishes of every aviation authority in Denver, Mayor Stapleton purchased the Sand Creek site from his friend H. Brown Cannon. In purchasing the site, the mayor paid off a political debt of many years' standing."

On page six of the same edition of the *Denver Post*, the paper ran a letter to the editor from a Henry V. Johnson, a Denver citizen, who also opposed the airport. He wrote: "I am informed by a number of Denver real estate men that this particular tract of land is not worth half of the $125,000 that is proposed to be paid for it . . . I am also informed that the airplane men say they will not use it even if the city should make the absurd mistake of buying it."

The *Denver Post* was the most powerful opponent to Stapleton and his plans for an airport. The paper was the first to call the project "Stapleton's Folly" and Simpleton's Sand Dunes," and refer to the mayor as "King Ben." Even considering the more melodramatic newspaper styles of the 1920s, the *Post* came dangerously close to libel and slander many times during the coverage of the airport project.

On the morning of the city council's appropriation meeting, the *Rocky Mountain News* reported that the city attorney, Thomas H. Gibson, had declared that the city did have the authority to purchase and operate an airport. As proof, Gibson cited the section of the state constitution which had granted Denver's city charter. This section, he said, gave the city the power to purchase and maintain any city utility from the general city fund. "The airport," he continued, "is as properly included within park purposes as tourist camps and other recreational objects."

Even with the substantial opposition to the airport, Stapleton's political influence was simply too strong to be overridden. On the evening of March 25, 1928, the city council appropriated $175,000 for the purchase of the Sand Creek site. Nine months later, after all parcels of the site were purchased, the total bill for the acquisition was $143,013.37. The remaining $32,000 of acquisition money was added to the 1929 budget of $175,000, which the city had already set aside for the construction of a new airport.

## Denver Builds an Airport

Now that the land was purchased, construction was begun immediately. Plans for the airport had undergone many changes during the year it had taken the city council to act and buy the land. Peck's original design of a four-runway airport was changed, and the plans for the airport that were finally used were drafted by H. S. Crocker of the parks department. The planned hangar was enlarged three times during the design stage to incorporate the larger fuselages and wingspans of newly developed airplanes.

From the very beginning, Stapleton wanted the airport to obtain the highest aviation rating from the Department of Commerce; that is, the A-1-A. To receive such a rating, one of the department's recommendations was that airports constructed at high altitudes should have runways of at least 3,300 feet. When the Denver Municipal Airport was built, these specifications were followed. The two major runways (there were also two diagonal runways) were more than the specified 3,300 feet: the north-south runway was 4,050 feet and the east-west runway extended 4,650 feet. Both had a gravel topping and an elaborate system of tiling installed along their sides to ensure proper drainage during inclement weather.

A unique and elaborate lighting system was installed at the new airport by the Public Service Company of Colorado. On top of the administration building was a high intensity light that pilots could see from miles away, called the "Eye of Denver." Another high intensity light was housed in a small structure between the administration building and the hangar. This was a special landing light which projected a beam of light in a 180-degree arc, exactly six feet off the ground. When a pilot was making a night landing, he would know when his plane was six feet from the ground when the beam hit the plane. Reports state that the beam worked well except when dust was blowing around the airport. The reflection of light off the dust particles obscured the ground from landing pilots.

The construction of the buildings and runways was completed in the spring and summer of 1929. There was an administration building; a hangar with a lean-to

maintenance shop attached; and a small building that housed the fire-fighting equipment, ambulance and central heating plant, which supplied heat to all the buildings.

The administration building was a three-story structure of brick and steel. On the first floor was a lobby and waiting room, a restaurant, a ladies lounge, some mail and baggage rooms and lavatories. The second floor housed the administrative offices, including the airport manager's private office and three suites of offices available on lease for transportation companies. The second floor also furnished pilots with three sleeping rooms, lavatories, showers, baths and a radio room. The cupola third floor held a meteorological station which Denver hoped would be taken over by the federal government and made into a regular government forecasting station. Until that happened, weather information was received from the downtown main Post Office, then transmitted to the pilots.

The hangar building was a huge structure for its time, 121 feet by 122 feet, and painted a bright orange so it could be seen readily by approaching pilots. The hangar was, reportedly, so large, "you could build a ship in it." The dedication program announced: "It [the hangar] will accommodate 12 of the largest type transport ships, and is especially designed to give clearance, afforded by but comparatively few other hangars, to not only the largest ships of today, but to the huge ships of the future." (A Boeing 747 has a wingspan of 195 feet and a length of 228 feet.)

The hangar that was built to last for several years served its purpose well: In the late 1940s it was moved to the western edge of the airfield for use by small, private planes; on October 11, 1964 it was moved and used by Clinton Aviation until 1971, when it was finally razed. Even with this huge hangar, the dedication program reflected the growing need for more hangar space, "It is even now apparent that additional hangar and shop facilities will have to be provided in the near future."

By late summer/early autumn of 1929, the Denver Municipal Airport had cost Denver approximately $430,000 in land acquisition, preparation and construction but was ready for operation. The dedication program grandly announced that in return for the money spent on the airport:

> Denver citizens have the knowledge that their city boasts one of the finest airports in the land. That this achievement in building places it in the forefront of progressive cities which are meeting the problems arising from the rapid development of a new method of commercial transportation; and that its fame will be advanced wherever planes land or take off, which means nearly every spot on the face of the globe.

Construction of the administration, or terminal, building for the new Denver Municipal Airport began in spring of 1929. Courtesy of the Colorado Historical Society.

By June 1929 the new hangar was taking shape. Courtesy of the Colorado Historical Society.

By summer 1929, the terminal building was complete. It housed a lobby, waiting room, restaurant, ladies lounge, mail and baggage rooms, and lavatories on the first floor. The second floor held the airport's administrative offices and three suites of offices that were leased to airline companies. A meteorological station took up the cupola third floor. Courtesy of the Western History Department, Denver Public Library.

*On August 14, 1929, a month and a half before the official opening of the new airport, Denver residents came in droves to view a row of Army bombers. Courtesy of the* Denver Post.

On September 22, 1929, a month before the official dedication, the *Rocky Mountain News* reported three air carrier firms were preparing to open offices at the Denver Municipal Airport: Western Air Express (which carried airmail on the Cheyenne-Denver-Pueblo route and had been previously using Lowry Air Field); U.S. Airways, Inc. (which flew the mail from Denver to Kansas City); and Mid-Continent Express (which had just begun service between Denver and El Paso, with coast-to-coast connections at Albuquerque, New Mexico).

## Denver's Place in the Sun

With the airport already functioning, the opening ceremonies were prepared by Stapleton, Vail and the city council's committees and subcommittees. The dedication would take place over a four-day period, October 17–20, 1929. By September of 1929, the subcommittees were meeting every day, and politicians

and businessmen alike were trying to drum up interest across the country.

On September 30, the *Rocky Mountain News* previewed the planned ceremonies. There would be military and civilian aerial races, planes from all over the country, a lighting ceremony in conjunction with the nation's celebration of Light's Golden Jubilee commemorating Thomas Edison's invention, appearances by politicians and leading citizens, and a dramatic aerial bombing of a "village" by the Colorado 120th National Guard Squadron. The races would be held under the rules of the National Aeronautical Association. The article also reported Mayor Stapleton had received a telegram from Major General C. W. Bridges of the War Department in Washington. Bridges wired that the War Department would order as many planes as possible to attend the ceremonies from various airfields in Texas. It was mentioned that the Army Air Corps planes would participate in the ceremonies on Friday and Saturday, but they could not fly exhibitions on Sunday because War Department

# ON THE AIR MAP AT LAST

*Heralding the birth of the new airport, the* Rocky Mountain News *ran this cartoon on October 17, 1929. Excerpt from the* Rocky Mountain News, *courtesy of the Colorado Historical Society.*

*Denver Municipal's ambulance. Courtesy of the Colorado Historical Society.*

*The 15 airport attendants and the airport's mascot on October 17, 1929. Courtesy of the* Denver Post.

In 1929 Mid-Continent Express was welcomed to the new Denver Airport as one of only three major airline companies to establish offices there. The other two were Western Air Express and U.S. Airways, Inc. Courtesy of the Western History Department, Denver Public Library.

The high intensity light that stood just northeast of the terminal aided in night landings. It cast a high intensity beam of light exactly six feet off the ground across the field. When a plane hit the beam, the pilot knew he was six feet off the ground. Courtesy of the Western History Department, Denver Public Library.

regulations forbid exhibition flying on the Sabbath. The article even mentioned that the U.S. Navy's dirigible, *Los Angeles*, might appear, and that "virtually every leading businessman in Denver has wired to Washington, asking for the presence of the mighty airship" (no such appearance happened, however).

Publicity for the event was so widespread that every airplane manufacturer in Colorado and many from around the country had promised to have a plane participate. The famous *Mystery Ship* was supposed to attend. This plane had been built by the Travelair Company and had flown in the national air races held in August in Cleveland. It had thrilled the crowds with its "speed and ease of handling."

The opposition to the airport that had been voiced in 1927 and 1928 was forgotten. Even the *Denver Post* was now singing the praises of the new airport. Everyone in Denver was proud of the new facility and wanted the country to know about it.

In the early publicity of the opening ceremonies, Denver Municipal Airport was called the "Seaport of the Sky," the dedication program called it the "Union Station of the Air," and the dedication itself was called the "Festival of the Skies." The dedication program also stated, "The new Municipal Airport clinches Denver's place in the sun." Whatever name was used, though, everyone in the surrounding area and much of the western United States waited anxiously for the festivities to begin.

## Opening Ceremonies

### Thursday, October 17, 1929

The city had prepared well for the opening ceremonies. There were numerous civilian and military aerial contests offering more than $5,000 in prize money. The airport was temporarily fenced off (by this time fences used to restrain crowds were called "Lindbergh fences" because of the necessity for fences to restrain crowds whenever Lindbergh appeared in public), and there were 200 policemen, 200 firemen, 150 workmen and 400 citizen volunteers prepared to maintain order and help the ceremonies go smoothly. A field hospital was set up in the administration building for emergencies, staffed by Denver General Hospital personnel. There was parking for 15,000 cars around the sand dunes, which ringed the airport.

On the first morning hundreds of people were on hand at eight o'clock to gawk at the flaming orange hangar and the early arrivals in the "On-to-Denver" race, the first scheduled event of the four-day celebration. The On-to-Denver race had caused a lively interest in Denver during the previous week because of its unique nature and rules.

The race rules stated an airplane had to start from at least 200 miles away and had to arrive at the Municipal Airport between 8:00 A.M. and 12:00 midnight on October 17. A point system was used to compensate for different mileages, types of engine and aircraft and number of passengers carried. To enter, a pilot had only to announce his intention just before takeoff, with two responsible people certifying in writing the time of departure and the home field.

Because of this specific ruling, many pilots did not announce their intentions early "to prevent opposition pilots from learning of their coming." This led to a great deal of speculation as to who was coming and from where. The *Rocky Mountain News* related this speculation in a subheadline used on October 16, 1929, "'On-to-Denver' Race Starts at Daybreak; 'Dark Horses' Cause Riot of Conjecture; Many Pilots Are Believed to Be Proceeding in Secrecy."

In addition to the planes flying to Denver in the On-to-Denver race, military and civilian planes were expected to arrive from across the country. U.S. Army Air Corps planes were reported on their way from Brooks Field, Duncan Field, Ft. Crockett Field and Kelly Field in Texas; and from Rockwell Field in California. Throughout the day, Curtiss attack and pursuit planes, Douglas observation planes and heavy bombers began arriving.

The first entry to arrive in the On-to-Denver race was W. A. Williams who, with his passenger Vernon Cheever, arrived at 8:53 A.M. from McCook, Nebraska. Williams had flown a distance of 240 miles with an average speed of 127.8 miles per hour.

There were no scheduled events on this first day of the ceremonies, but there was much to see for the estimated 15,000 people who came to the field. The crowd looked over the buildings and hangar and watched the planes that were arriving continually. At sunset, an impromptu parade of cars began driving around the borders of the airport. The flood and border lights were switched on to entertain the parade, which lasted until midnight.

### Friday, October 18, 1929

By Friday, 60 planes had arrived at the airport. Among them was a Boeing tri-motor, 18-passenger plane. It had flown 11 passengers from Cheyenne and was reported to be the third largest airplane in the world and the second largest ever built in the United States. Meals were served while in flight, and it was likened to "the finest Pullman car." Army pilots and planes performed aerial stunts between races to thrill the crowd, and planes in the speed races flew as fast as 180 miles an hour.

The second day's events consisted of formation flying for military pilots only, a pony express race, a speed race

*On the first day of the four-day opening celebration, thousands watched as one of the planes taking part in the races and events comes in for what seems to be a precarious landing. Courtesy of Stapleton International Airport.*

*A row of Army planes await their pilots. Army and private planes came from as far away as Texas and California to participate in the races. Courtesy of the Colorado Aviation Historical Society.*

*A bird's eye view of the opening ceremonies. In the far, upper right-hand corner of this picture the Windsor Farm Dairy can be seen. Just below and to the left of the farm is the silhouette village that awaits the Army's bombing run. On the gravel runway planes kick up dust around the racing pylon. Hundreds of cars parked wherever space was available in the fields behind the airport. Courtesy of the Western History Department, Denver Public Library.*

*During the first three days of the ceremonies the crowds had to stand behind the "Lindbergh" fences. More than 200 policemen, 200 firemen, 150 workmen and 400 citizen volunteers were on hand to help the dedication go smoothly. Courtesy of the Colorado Historical Society.*

*The festivities did not end with the coming of night. Floodlights atop the hangar and terminal provided light for those who wanted to wander through and around the buildings. Courtesy of the Western History Department, Denver Public Library.*

*On a knoll east of the terminal building, spectators rest during the ceremonies. Courtesy of the Colorado Aviation Historical Society.*

for National Guard pilots, a precision landing contest and an altitude race for civilians only. Special events included a radio broadcast from an airplane in flight and the official lighting of the airport's $30,000 lighting system to mark the formal dedication of the airport.

The pony express race had pilots and planes flying around pylons, landing and exchanging parcels with a judge three times over a 10-mile course. The altitude races had planes racing to see which could climb up to 5,000 feet the fastest. After the altitude race was completed, the winner of the On-to-Denver race was announced. In first place was Everett Williams who piloted three passengers from Garden City, Kansas, to Denver in an Eaglerock Bullet. He received a first prize of $1,000.

From 3:15 to 3:30, KOA radio station broadcasted from a Mid-Continent Express plane 5,000 feet off the ground. Julian C. Riley was the announcer and Ralph Hansel (xylophonist) and Dick Roberts (banjo) performed for the crowd below. There was a special hookup between the plane and the loudspeakers atop the administration building so that the spectators could hear the broadcast.

The highlight of the second day was the official lighting of the airport after sunset by Governor William H. Adams. (Unfortunately, Mayor Stapleton, for whom the facility was later named, was at Presbyterian Hospital recuperating from pneumonia.) Governor Adams first had the hangar lights switched on, followed by the boundary lights; then the administration building was illuminated; and finally the landing beacon was turned on. With the completion of the lighting, the estimated crowd of 20,000 cheered continuously for five minutes. Governor Adams proclaimed the airport the "finest in America—one that will meet aviation's needs for years to come."

The first plane to take off from the lighted field was a Fokker Super-Universal owned by Mid-Continent. Another plane took off and the two were joined in flight by a third plane that had just arrived for the ceremonies. All three planes flashed their lights at the crowd below, with one of them sending Morse code which signaled, "The combined pilots congratulate Denver on its new airport." The Fokker plane then voice-broadcasted a message that was fed through the loudspeakers below: "In the Denver Municipal Airport you have something of which to be proud. It is one of the best in the world. From the standpoint of lighting it is the best in the world."

Dick Crane, pilot of one of the three planes aloft, then dropped emergency flares from his plane and demonstrated an emergency night landing. Following

*During the three days of events, spectators witnessed many new and breath-taking things. But by far the most imaginative and thrilling was the bombing of the silhouette village erected on the southeast side of the north-south runway. On October 19, the third day of the dedication, thousands watched as Army pilots in open cockpit planes dove towards the village and hand-dropped explosives, destroying the village in only two passes. Courtesy of the* Denver Post.

him, the two other planes landed. With all three planes down, the lights were switched off for a fireworks display. The image of Thomas A. Edison sparked to life to commemorate Light's Golden Jubilee.

### Saturday, October 19, 1929

Saturday saw more speed racing, precision flying and altitude contests. At 10:00 A.M. a squadron of Army planes flew to the vicinity of Presbyterian Hospital and performed aerial stunts for Mayor Stapleton. On returning to the field, they once again performed stunts for the crowd.

Between races there was formation flying by groups of pilots for the audience. One such group was the Air Corps' "Yellowjackets" from Kelly Field in San Diego. The Yellowjackets were Lieutenants Carr, Smith and Taylor. They did barrell rolls, loops, slow rolls, flying upside down and "vicious dives at the ground, [which] brought the spectators to their toes in wonder at the daring of these Army birds," according to the *Denver Post.*

In the afternoon, 10 Curtiss pursuit planes performed aerial feats during halftime at the Colorado College-Denver University football game at the Denver University stadium. And at 3:00 P.M. all the Army planes then at Denver Municipal Airport took to the air for a formation review.

The highlight of Saturday's performance was the bombing of a "village" on the east side of the airport. The "village" was actually a silhouette of a castle that had been constructed for the performance. The newspapers had announced Major Bruce Kistler would lead his Colorado National Guard bombers in blowing up this village, but at the last minute, when three U.S. Air Corps Keystone bombers arrived from California, the honor of blowing up the village was given to them. An estimated 50,000 people were on hand to watch the event, and the *Rocky Mountain News* reported: "Twice, the death-dealing trio swept low across the field, each time dropping explosives. The 'village' crumpled, exploded and burst into flames."

As the last of the bombs exploded, the third day's ceremonies were over. A banquet that evening at the Brown Palace Hotel capped the day's celebration, with visiting aviators as the guests of honor.

### Sunday, October 20, 1929

For three days thousands of people had to watch the events, pilots and planes from behind the "Lindbergh fences." With no scheduled events on Sunday, an open house was declared and the gates to the Municipal Airport were finally opened to the crowd. William F. Wunderlick, manager of the airport, and two of his assistants were on hand to give guided tours of the facility. The more than 60 planes that had flown in the last three days of events and performances were parked along the runways. They were, as the *Rocky Mountain News* reported, "on display for the inevitable peek into the cockpit, the tapping of the wings and the feeling of the propeller."

An estimated 50,000 people showed up and an estimated 25,000 cars parked among the sand dunes that ringed the airport. Free flying trips were given to more than 1,000 people and 8 tramway buses operated from the field and the Park Hill rail line at East Twenty-third Avenue and Fairfax Street, carrying close to 4,500 people.

Because of the airport celebration, Governor Adams had proclaimed October 14-19 airmail week. The citizens had responded so enthusiastically that more airplanes had to be added to the usual Friday and Saturday night runs to Cheyenne. A *Denver Post* artist had designed a special cachet for airmail week and Light's Jubilee. More than 25,000 letters bore the cachet by the end of the airmail week.

Also during the celebration, the *Denver Post* reported on October 19 that Lieutenant Edmund Q. B. Henriques, the aviation manager of the new Hotel New Yorker in New York City, and H. F. Stevens, assistant manager of the hotel, had stopped in Denver on a tour around the country to gather aviation information for their hotel guests. They were trying to establish an aviation travel bureau similar to the steamship travel bureau at the hotel. The two men visited F. G. Bonfils, publisher of the *Denver Post* and "conveyed to him greetings from Mayor Jimmy Walker of New York City, who congratulated him on the part the *Post* had taken in promoting airmindedness in the West." This statement, ironically, was made about the same paper that had less than two years before suggested Denver had no right to purchase, build or operate an airport, and that Stapleton's purchasing of the Sand Creek site was simply to repay a political debt.

On the final day of the opening ceremonies, the Army Air Corps planes began departing to fly to their home fields and the crowds slowly, reluctantly, got in their cars and headed home.

Although the stock-market crash on October 29, 1929, stole the headlines from Denver's new airport only a week and a half later, Denver nonetheless had its airport. The foresight of a few had guaranteed Denver's place in the sun.

*Looking south from out of the hangar. Note the Eye of Denver atop the terminal building and the crowded parking lot behind the building. Courtesy of the Western History Department, Denver Public Library.*

# Chapter Two

With the opening of the airport, most people felt Denver's aviation standing was secure. The Municipal Airport boasted three relatively large airline companies and four local flying services operating from its ultra modern facilities. What more could be needed?

Farsighted city officials, however, like Mayor Stapleton, recognized the necessity of continually upgrading and expanding the airport's facilities to keep pace with the evolving aviation industry and the increasing number of passengers. These officials, as well as aviation enthusiasts throughout Colorado, knew that Denver must take on the task of developing Denver Municipal Airport into a regional air hub if the city wanted to become a part of the major aerial transportation lines of the United States. If this task was to be achieved, the airport had to continue to change with the new developments of the airplane as well as become financially independent of city revenues. Financial independence was especially important in early 1930 as the United States began feeling the effects of the depression that would later be known as the Great Depression.

In 1929, the Denver City Council had decided on an annual appropriation of $25,000 for the airport during the next few years. This money came from the city's general fund, and the facility was part of the Parks and Improvement Department. The manager of that department was the overseer of the airport, with an airport manager appointed to run the day-to-day operations. Because money for the airport came from city coffers, approval of all construction and expansion had to come from the city council. The plans for such changes were usually prepared by Denver's mayor, the airport manager and the manager of the Parks and Improvements Department, then proposed to the city council.

## A Shaky Beginning for a Young Airport

Because of the Great Depression and the fact that Denver had recently spent nearly half a million dollars to build the airport, 1930 was a year of waiting. Waiting to see the extent of aviation activity and revenues generated by Denver Municipal. At this critical time in

the airport's history, it was an economic fact that an airport that did not quickly pull its own financial weight was doomed, for the American people believed there were more important matters to spend money on than airports.

Denver Municipal Airport's revenues were generated by landing, storage and rental fees for the runways, hangars and office space. The bulk of the revenues came from the three airlines and four flying services operating from the airport. The three airline companies—Western Air Express, Mid-Continent Express and U.S. Airways—flew mail cargo and passengers along feeder routes. The four flying services—Western Flying Service, Ream's Flying Service, Brook's Flying Service and Morean Flying Service—offered charter flights, aerial photo taking, pilot instruction and sightseeing. In the last three months of 1929, these seven companies contributed the majority of the $1,919 collected and flew the bulk of the total air miles (145,000) in and out of Denver Municipal. Almost a year later, the *Rocky Mountain News* on November 4, 1930, gave its readers a report on the airport's financial progress. The first nine months of 1930 did not bode well for the airport, bringing in an average monthly income of only $700. If this situation had continued much longer, the airport's survival could have been jeopardized.

What saved Denver Municipal was a sudden jump in air activity during the last three months of 1930. In this period, air traffic increased to the point where the year's revenues exceeded the yearly city appropriation of $25,000, making Denver Municipal's first complete year of operation a profitable one. Takeoffs and landings in the last three months of 1930 jumped from the previous average of eight a day to thirty a day. The air miles flown in and out of Denver Municipal climbed to 1,627,000 and more than 18,000 pounds of airmail was dispatched from the airport—an 11-percent increase over the airmail handled in 1929. Even the small flying services reported substantial activity, with 90–100 instructional flights per week during 1930.

No single factor was attributed to this end-of-the-year jump in aviation activity. It is assumed that more planes and people came to Denver Municipal Airport as its name became better known. Whatever the reasons, though, the last three months of 1930 showed the people of Denver that their airport could become self-supportive, even during economic hard times.        .

Construction and improvements at Denver Municipal Airport during 1930 were minimal. The city council had appropriated $150,000 for a special construction fund, of which only $19,224 had been spent by November 1930. This money had been used for the purchase of an ambulance, a fire wagon, shop equipment and for receptions for the National Reliability Fliers and the Chamber of Commerce Goodwill Tour. By the end of 1930, because of the increase in air traffic, more landing lights and beacons were installed to cover 365 acres—up from the 345 acres originally lit. Also, through the supervision of the city landscape architect, S. R. DeBoer, a slight mound was built in front of the administration building with "Denver" embossed on it, and curbing was installed along all streets leading to the airport.

With the increase in air activity by the end of 1930, plans were made to construct a new lounge in the administration building, for a cost of $40,000, and a new hangar was discussed to store and repair the increasing number of aircraft using the airport. Airport manager Wunderlich and his staff of 40, including engineers, clerks, mechanics and general helpers, were kept busy.

In 1930, Denver Municipal also received the coveted top rating of A-1-A from the Department of Commerce, the designation Mayor Stapleton had hoped for. The only other airport in the country, at the time, to receive this highest rating was the facility in Pontiac, Michigan.

With this top rating, the financial boom in the last three months of 1930, and the discussion of a new hangar and lounge, Denver Municipal Airport flew into 1931 with great expectations. It was going to be a big year.

## 1931—Improvements Are Made

By January 1931, plans for improvements at the airport were finalized. Wunderlich announced to the press that there would be a new hangar, larger than the original one; a car garage for use by airfield workers, airline officials and out-going passengers; and a "dope" shed where repairs would be made on any broken canvas wings. Wunderlich explained that there was currently $112,434 in the permanent improvement fund for the airport, which would cover all new construction. The airport was gearing up through these improvements to satisfy the growing needs of increased air traffic in and out of Denver Municipal Airport.

By September of 1931 the new hangar was ready for use. It had cost the city $70,000 to build but was considered one of the most modern facilities in the country. It could house 16 average-sized planes and was 150 feet long by 100 feet deep. The front door was 22 feet high and 150 feet long—the largest door of its kind

in the country. Operated electrically, it could be opened in 35 seconds, allowing quick evacuation of planes in an emergency. The building was of steel and concrete design with a 20-by-100 foot lean-to behind it. The city expected the yearly rental of the hangar to generate approximately $7,500. With the new hangar, Denver Municipal had a storage capacity of 32 aircraft.

Even though the new hangar was exciting aviation news for Denver citizens, the most important event of the year for the airport came from Western Air Express. Western announced in April 1931 that 2,000 miles of new routes through Denver were being established, connecting the city with Fort Worth, Dallas, Tulsa, Oklahoma City and Amarillo. To many in Denver, this was considered an important step in establishing the city as a regional transportation center. The *Denver Post* on April 9, stated, "Its [Western Express'] growing system is helping to closely knit the states of the Rocky Mountain league, and more strongly establishes Denver as a hub of aerial activities."

## Washington Steps Into Aviation Once Again

While Denver's airport was growing and building for the future, important decisions by lawmakers in Washington were being made that would directly affect the future growth of airline companies and indirectly affect the prosperity of Denver's Municipal Airport.

Although passenger revenues were increasing almost daily for most airline companies, many still depended heavily on revenues generated from flying mail for the Post Office. The flying of mail was regulated by government contracts under the control of the U.S. Post Office. In 1930, Congress passed the Watres Mail Act which directed the Post Office to unify the air transportation industry in order to cut what some thought was wasteful competition. The legislators felt that if the industry could be consolidated, it would better serve the Post Office as well as the growing number of air travelers. Walter F. Brown, then postmaster general under Herbert Hoover, forced consolidation of the airlines by awarding contracts for certain major routes to only one company. Previously, a major route might have been handled by a number of small airlines flying pieces of the route. Aviation companies quickly realized that merging with each other might be the only means of economic survival. This was the case with Western Air Express and Transcontinental Air Transport, who merged to form a company that later became known as Trans World Airlines (TWA). By 1932, the law's effect had been felt nationwide: only 32 commercial airline companies were still flying, down from 43 in 1930.

If this had been the last of governmental interference many airlines could have weathered the storm.

*Looking east from out of the hangar. Courtesy of the Western History Department, Denver Public Library.*

*Airport attendants assist in the moving of an airplane. Courtesy of the* Denver Post.

*Denver Municipal Airport in 1930. Courtesy of the Western History Department, Denver Public Library. Courtesy of the Colorado Historical Society.*

*The fuel truck serviced many different planes, from the small open cockpit ones to this Boeing Air Transport. Courtesy of the Western History Department, Denver Public Library.*

On June 3, 1931, Amelia Erhart, at the invitation of F. G. Bonfils (owner of the Denver Post), stopped at Denver Municipal Airport on her cross country flight of the "autogiro." The autogiro was invented by a Spaniard and was the precursor of the helicopter. Courtesy of the Colorado Aviation Historical Society.

By 1931 a second hangar had been constructed and a tarmac encompassed all three main structures. The new hangar had an electric door 22 feet high and 150 feet long, the largest door of its kind in the country (opposite, above). Courtesy of the Colorado Historical Society.

In the 1930s it was just a simple stroll out of the terminal building and into a waiting passenger plane (opposite, below). Courtesy of Western Airlines.

Unfortunately, in 1934 a scandal in the airline industry was unearthed over the awarding of airmail contracts. Certain airlines had been awarded lucrative contracts, even though other firms had submitted lower bids. Brigadier General William (Billy) Mitchell, famous World War I flying ace, lent support to the accusations of aviation corruption when he testified in front of the House Post Office Committee in March 1934. As reported by the *Rocky Mountain News*, March 22, he stated, "Aviation development in America lagged behind Europe because commercial aviation 'is in the hands of the gang that got the airmail contracts.'"

President Roosevelt, upon being informed of the scandal, immediately cancelled all airmail contracts and ordered the U.S. Army Air Corps to fly the mail. This was a death blow to many airlines that had relied solely on

*In 1932 new asbestos suits came to Denver Municipal Airport for use in aviation fires (opposite, above). Courtesy of the* Denver Post.

*The 1935 Airshow (opposite, below). Courtesy of the* Denver Post.

*George E. Cranmer, manager of Improvements and Parks from 1935-1947 did a great deal in conjunction with Mayor Stapleton to ensure the airport grew to meet the changing needs and demands of aviation in the critical 1930s and 1940s. Courtesy of the Western History Department, Denver Public Library.*

airmail contracts for their incomes. By 1938, there were only 16 airline companies in existence.

Problems arose, however, with the new airmail arrangement. The U.S. Army Air Corps had as much luck flying the mail in 1934 as it had in 1918-1919. Within a few months of compliance with Roosevelt's orders, the Air Corps had 16 airplane accidents. Such ineptitude led Congress to quickly pass the Air Mail Act of 1934, which once again returned the airmail service to private contractors.

This time, however, there were certain stipulations the airlines had to comply with before receiving airmail contracts. No airline executive who had been in office during the old contracts could continue working for the same airline company. As a result of this, many executives simply resigned and were rehired by other airline companies, leaving the commercial aviation leadership basically intact. Also, no airline company could hold a majority interest in an airline manufacturing company. This portion of the bill separating airline manufacturing from transportation operations was part of the government's overall antitrust actions of the 1930s. Another stipulation to the bill was that no airline company that held a previous airmail contract could bid on the new ones. The loophole that saved many airlines was that they needed only to reorganize under a different name to be able to bid on the new contracts.

Throughout the controversy over the airmail contracts, Denver airport and city officials waited to see what effect the legislation would have on the airport's profits and future growth. Because the law dealt only with the commercial air carriers, Denver's local flying services were not affected, which kept a steady flow of revenues coming in. However, the law did affect Western Air Express, the largest airline at Denver Municipal. With the cancelling of the airmail contracts in 1934, Western lost its authority to fly into Denver. The airline did not serve Denver again until 1944 when it purchased Inland Airlines.

The law also affected the immediate, anticipated growth of the airport during the early 1930s. The airline companies that had been expanding and growing into new locations and new routes were severely cut back by the government. The expected growth of major air carriers into Denver Municipal during the early 1930s simply did not happen. The airport would have to wait until 1937 before attracting major commercial carriers to take Western's place.

But there were some benefits from the new law passed by Congress in 1934. Smaller airline companies began to expand during this period because of the cutbacks the larger companies were experiencing. Wyoming Air Service, a small commercial carrier, began flying the Denver-Colorado Springs-Pueblo route in 1934; and Varney Air Lines, another commercial carrier, began flying from Denver to Mexico on July 15, 1934.

## Plans for a Denver Army Air Base Develop

Air-minded citizens of Denver were watching Denver Municipal Airport, as well as developments in Washington, in their continuing struggles to make the city an aerial center. If the Municipal Airport could not do the whole job for them, they would welcome any other form of help that would give Denver national aviation exposure and recognition.

In 1934, U.S. Congressman J. Mark Wilcox of Florida, testifying before a federal aviation committee called for 20 air bases to be built around the country for national air defense. In light of Adolf Hitler's rise to power in Germany and Japan's continued belligerence toward China, most world powers were enlarging their air forces as the plane proved to be an efficient machine of war. In the United States, Wilcox was one of many who advocated a stronger U.S. aerial defense. Wilcox's plan called for the 20 air bases to be placed around U.S. borders with a few strategically placed inland. After testifying, Wilcox called the Denver Chamber of Commerce and told them he believed one of the inland bases should be placed in Denver. Would they help support the effort to get an air base in Denver?

Believing an air base would help establish the city as an important air hub and generate much needed revenues and jobs, the Chamber of Commerce gave its complete support and sent a delegation to Washington. The delegation told Congress that because the largest supply of gold in the country was in the Denver Federal Mint (Ft. Knox's gold depository was established by the Government in 1935), the city was a prime target for attack in the event of war. Denver could be attacked, the delegation reasoned, only from the air; therefore, it needed a strong aerial defense. Another point mentioned by the delegation was that Denver already had Fitzsimmon General Hospital and Fort Logan—both Army installations—so it would be only natural to also house an Army air base in Denver.

In mid-1937, the decision was made to establish the Western Technical Training Command of the U.S. Army Air Corps in Denver. The air base would be called Lowry Field in honor of Frances Brown Lowry, a Denver man killed in action in France during World War I. (Lowry Air Field, which operated from 1924 to 1948 should not be confused with the U.S. Army installation, Lowry Field.) Estimated to cost the government $5 million, the installation would ultimately house 100 attack planes, a number of blimps, a dirigible mooring and classroom facilities for aerial instruction.

Denver's victory was not, however, without cost. To ensure the base's location, the city council told Washington it would donate the land for the base. Denver citizens had passed a bond issue earlier to raise the needed funds to purchase the land, located around the Agnes (Phipps) Memorial Sanatorium and owned by former U.S. Senator L. C. Phipps. Denver had also agreed to supply the Air Corps with a bombing range within 50 miles of the city.

Although the $5 million to build Lowry would not be appropriated until 1938, Denver made arrangements for the Air Corps to begin training classes in the Sanatorium and to store their aircraft at Denver Municipal Airport.

## Back at Denver Municipal Airport

Immediately following the 1934 airmail scandal and subsequent legislation, Denver Municipal did little to improve or expand its facilities, for commercial aviation was almost at a standstill. In 1935, the city did install a public address system at the airport. It was placed atop the administration building and was reported by the *Rocky Mountain News* to be able to "throw a human voice three miles and give orders to planes in full flight." The system was also used to play music and make announcements during air shows.

The new PA system was put to its first real test during the July 4-6 Air Show in 1936. This event was actually two shows in one: the National Balloon Races, staged for the first time in Denver, and the Mile High Air Races. The balloonists were trying for distance from Denver Municipal and began leaving the airport Friday evening before the Mile High Races started. There were five balloons in the race: two Navy balloons, an Army Air Corps balloon, a Goodyear Tire balloon (called the *Goodyear X*), and the Cleveland Great Lakes Exposition balloon. The balloons sailed across the countryside during the night and the results were announced during the next two days of airplane events.

Also staged on Friday afternoon and early evening was practice flying by Major Al Williams, a former U.S. Navy test pilot and current commander of the Scripps–Howard Junior Aviators group. Williams put his plane through barrel rolls, power dives and inverted flying for the spectators who had come to the airport a day early hoping for such an event. Williams had a two-way radio in his plane connected to the airport's PA system, and as he went through his drills he talked to the crowd, explaining each move.

The next day—the first official day of the races—20,000 people showed up to watch the aerial thrills. There were speed races, precision flying and daredevil aerial teams. One such team was the Hollywood Hawks, a movie stunt team who flew through their stunts at more than 200 MPH. There were novelty races and events like the "Pants Off" race and the "Crazy Flight, or what not to do in an airplane" event. The Pants Off race had pilots loop the field the first time, land and remove their pants, loop the field again, put their pants back on

*The 1936 July 4-6 Airshow was actually two shows in one: The National Balloon Races, and the Mile High Air Races.
The balloon race featured five balloons, including the "Goodyear X." The airplane races included the "Pants Off"
race, the "Crazy Flight," and aerobatics by the Hollywood Hawks flying team. Courtesy of the Western History
Department, Denver Public Library.*

and lap the course one last time to the finish line. The women aviators (who were always a big part of any air show, for their numbers were increasing constantly) had red bloomers on under their pants for the Pants Off race.

The Crazy Flight event was staged by the Hollywood Hawks. A pilot was announced as a student attempting his first flight. As the *Rocky Mountain News* reported: "He started with a merry-go-round on the field. Then he stalled, missed a crash by an eye lash, dipped and wheeled. Six times he tried to land, only to bounce again into the air like a pancake gone crazy."

Also included in the day's events was a Pikes Peak–Cheyenne Mountain speed and efficiency race where commercial planes raced from the municipal field to Colorado Springs—circling Pikes Peak and Cheyenne Mountain—then back. There were also exhibitions of parachuting, with both men and women

participating. One woman's first chute only partially opened and, to the stunned crowd, it seemed that she just barely managed to get the second chute open in time. Still, she almost landed in the press box that was part of the grandstand.

During the first day, the balloon race results were announced. The U.S. Army balloon had the misfortune of crashing and burning on a farm near Elizabeth, Colorado, while the rest of the balloons, reportedly, landed inside the state. These reports, however, proved inaccurate, for the *Goodyear X* landed the next day near Presho, South Dakota, 385 miles from Denver—not a new U.S. record (the record was 571 miles), but good enough to win the race.

Mayor Stapleton took his first airplane flight during the three-day air show announcing the occasion over the airport's PA system. His trip was in a plane owned by Frank Phillips, an oil company president from

Bartlesville, Oklahoma. The trip lasted 20 minutes, giving Stapleton his first aerial view of the city he loved.

An interesting record of the crowd was reported by a *Rocky Mountain News* writer on July 6. He wrote:

> The crowd presented an interesting cross-section glimpse of Colorado. On the lawn near the Administration building were farmers with big families from Northern Colorado, who came to Denver with picnic lunches to make a day of it. Hundreds of young office workers and clerks took their best girls to the races to get the heart throbs and thrill of a lifetime. The boxes held the pick of Denver society and city and state officials.

## Hangars Built, Runways Reconditioned, Safety Measures Taken

In the mid- to late 1930s construction and improvements were made to accommodate the increasing activity at Denver Municipal. Hangars were a large part of the improvements. Denver Municipal originally had one hangar with a second built in 1931. In March 1936, the Colorado National Guard, which had been stationed at Lowry Air Field relocated to the more modern Denver Municipal Airport. The Works Progress Administration (WPA) moved the guard's hangar with federal and state funds. In 1937, another Colorado National Guard hangar was being constructed at the municipal airport when the state ran out of funds to complete the job. Denver agreed to take over the hangar for the cost of finishing it plus the ultimate reimbursement of the state funds already spent. When the hangar was completed at the end of 1937, half of the building was rented to the U.S. Air Corps until Lowry air base was completed and the other half was used by commercial airlines. The building was 120-by-149 feet.

Hangars were not, however, the only facility that received attention. The two main runways were reconditioned and paved: the north-south runway in 1937 and the east-west runway in 1938. This was done to accommodate the newer, heavier aircraft being built around the country. Another improvement was the remodeling of the old fire station located just south of the administration building, converting the fire station into a restaurant to serve the growing number of both passengers and airfield personnel. A new fire station was built further south of the administration building.

Air safety was another concern of airport personnel during the late 1930s. A special radio transmitting beam was being planned during 1937, although the beam would not be installed and operating until March 1938. Also to improve night flying to and from Denver, airway lights became functional in 1937 between Denver, Colorado Springs and Pueblo. These lights were positioned approximately 10 miles apart along the route. The lights had actually been installed several years before but had fallen into disrepair during the last two years due to lack of funds. In 1937, the Department of Commerce took on the task of making them operational again, declaring they would be on from sunset to sunrise.

## Denver Municipal Attracts Major Air Carriers

Because of these improvements, in 1937 Denver Municipal Airport again received a top rating from the Department of Commerce. This rating was important for it helped attract new airline companies to the airport, and new airlines meant better aviation service, increased airport revenues and a step closer to regional aviation importance and national recognition.

In the aviation industry, there were three major types of airline companies: trunk line companies, feeder or local service airlines and regular cargo carriers. The trunk line companies served primarily major cities over long distances, carrying mail, passengers and cargo. The feeder airlines, carrying mail, passengers and cargo, served the smaller cities and connected them with the trunk line cities. Cargo carriers carried only cargo to both the major and minor cities.

Although Denver needed to attract all three types of airlines, it especially wanted the trunk line carriers to use Denver Municipal, for they would supply the airport with a constant flow of revenue while providing steady airmail and passenger service. Also, if Denver Municipal could attract trunk line carriers, feeder airlines would surely follow in order to link themselves with the major routes flown by the trunk lines.

Since the airport's beginnings in 1929, Western had been the only trunk line company which had served Denver. In 1934, when the government cancelled all airmail contracts, Western had lost its authority into Denver, leaving the airport without a trunk line carrier. (Western returned to Denver on May 27, 1944, when it absorbed Inland Airlines, which then became the Inland Division of Western.) In 1937, Denver did, however, attract two trunk line carriers: United and Continental. For Denver Municipal to get two trunk line companies in the same year was a windfall.

United Airlines officially came to Denver on May 15, 1937, with its first regularly scheduled flight between Denver and Cheyenne—a route it had purchased from Wyoming Air Service. But United had actually been flying into Denver since 1935 under a lease agreement with Wyoming Air Service using Wyoming's B-247s. On December 23, 1936, at the insistence of Denver businessmen and citizens, United applied to the Post Office to have Denver designated as a regular airmail

*Courtesy of the* Denver Post.

*On May 16, 1937, coast-to-coast, one-carrier service began through United Airlines, heralding an important change in Denver Municipal's status as an airport. Courtesy of the Western History Department, Denver Public Library.*

stop on the transcontinental route. Before this time, the Denver–Cheyenne route had been merely a spur line off the main route. By May 11, 1937, the application was approved and four days later United began regular service from Denver to both coasts via Cheyenne. United also established, at the same time, a route from Denver to Grand Island, Nebraska. By adding these two routes to its already vast system, United made Denver—for the first time—a city with coast-to-coast, one company service. This news made headlines in both of Denver's major newspapers, for it was viewed as another step closer to regional and national importance.

Continental Airlines also made a big contribution to Denver's aviation standing in 1937. The airline had been operating the route from El Paso, Texas, north to Pueblo. On May 14, 1937, Continental purchased Wyoming Air Service's southern route, Denver–Colorado Springs–Pueblo, (in conjunction with United's purchase of the Denver–Cheyenne route). This was the first time Denver was connected to El Paso by one company. By the end of the year, Continental—believing in the airport's present and future importance—moved its headquarters from El Paso to Denver Municipal. As the *Rocky Mountain News* reported on January 1, 1938, "For many years, Denver's future as an air center seemed limited, because of the barrier to air travel that the high mountain ranges formed west of the city." But all this was changed, the paper continued, with the decisions of United and Continental to begin using the Denver Municipal Airport.

With these two new carriers serving Denver, a great optimism and sense of celebration prevailed among the citizens who turned out to see the 1937 Air Show. Held on Sunday, September 13, and sponsored by the Rocky Mountain Chapter of the National Aeronautical Association and the Aviation Committee of the Denver Chamber of Commerce, it attracted more than 50,000 spectators.

The show was scheduled from 1:30–5:45 P.M., and the kickoff was an aerial parade over the city of all participating planes, including some from Continental and United. There were parachutists, a "Dog Fight" by two Colorado National Guard pilots and planes, the Pikes Peak race, spot landing contests, the now famous Pants Off race and a balloon-busting contest where flyers tried to pop gas filled balloons with their planes.

## 1938—A Big Year for Denver Municipal Airport

The year 1938 was an important one for the airport because of the changes that took place at the field as well as the progress that was made in recognition of

Denver as an important air center. To start the year, on April 19, the *Denver Post* reported the city would become the new district headquarters for the airport section of the U.S. Bureau of Air Commerce. This district office handled all construction and improvement of the 108 airports in Colorado, Utah, Wyoming and New Mexico. It moved to Denver from Salt Lake City because Denver was more centrally located for the upcoming improvements and construction of certain airports in the four-state region.

Another important federal action in 1938 that would have an effect on Denver Municipal, as well as all aviation, was the birth of the Civil Aeronautics Authority (CAA) from the Civil Aeronautics Act of 1938. The CAA (and later, in 1940, the Civil Aeronautics Board, CAB) was to take the place of the numerous government agencies previously controlling the aviation industry. The CAA was in charge of economic controls for airlines, approval of fares, routes and scheduling. Before the CAA, the Interstate Commerce Commission (ICC) had regulated rates and the Department of Commerce had established equipment specifications and approved routes.

The establishment of the CAA caused a stir in the aviation industry, for it was thought that this new agency might bring about important changes. In August 1938, W. P. Redding, the Washington representative of the Denver Chamber of Commerce and executive secretary of the Interstate Airways Committee, had attended the installation of the new CAA in Washington. Upon his return, he reported that Denver was to become an important air center through the new CAA. A provision of the Civil Aeronautics Act, Redding explained to the *Denver Post* on August 14, empowered the group to recommend congressional appropriations for improvements of key airports around the country. Redding said: "Denver stands high on the list of cities with important airports that should have the finest and most modern equipment. Under the new authority, that will be possible."

By early 1938, construction was once again being done at Denver Municipal Airport. Under WPA projects, the two major runways (north-south and east-west) were being extended and paved with asphalt to handle the new, larger planes that needed longer and stronger runways. The east-west runway would be extended to 5,200 feet and the north-south to 6,500 feet. Both runways would be 150 feet wide with 75-foot shoulders of leveled ground, making them 300 feet wide. The runway extensions were only possible through acquisition of land by the city. Two parcels were bought, 21 acres and 150 acres, which extended the boundaries of the airport north from Thirty-second Avenue and south from East Twenty-sixth Avenue to East Twenty-third Avenue.

*In early 1938 Denver Municipal Airport's first control tower, called the "Matchbox," became functional and was operated by the CAA. Courtesy of the* Denver Post.

## Denver Municipal Gets a Control Tower

Air traffic continued to increase, not only at Denver Municipal but around the entire area. Because of aircraft congestion, especially from private planes, the Colorado National Guard went so far in 1938 as to call for the state legislature to pass a law prohibiting night flying by private operators and all flying over Denver. With the government's Lowry Field becoming operational just north of Denver Municipal, there was talk of possible midair collisions and crashes in the confusion of so many planes taking off and landing from approximately the same area.

The problem became so pronounced that the manager of the Parks and Improvements Department, George E. Cranmer, who was in charge of the airport, appointed an aviation committee to study the problem. The committee, made up of aviation experts from the private, commercial and military sectors, had the job of establishing some rules of air traffic that would be submitted to the Department of Air Commerce for approval. There was a rumor of a possible control tower with city paid dispatchers on duty at all times to govern all takeoffs and landings at the three major airfields in the area: Denver Municipal, Lowry and Lowry's auxiliary field located several miles east of Denver, near Watkins.

By March 1938, a decision had been reached and approval received from the CAA for a trafic tower atop the Denver Municipal's administration building. The *Denver Post* reported on March 8, 1938: "Airplane traffic at the municipal airport has become so extensive and congested recently that as a safety measure it was deemed advisable to establish a control system with a 'cop' in charge. He will regulate incoming and outbound planes by two-way radio communication and a portable red and green traffic light."

A control tower of this sort was not that new to the industry. In 1935, the first control tower was erected and put into operation at the Newark, New Jersey, airport. In 1936, a few major airlines set up their own traffic control offices at three major airports. By July 1936, however, the government had taken over the duty of traffic control and placed it under the direction of the Department of Commerce's Bureau of Air Commerce, from which the new CAA took over in 1938.

Denver Municipal's "control tower" was a structure six feet high atop the administration building called the "matchbox." It was operated from 7:00 A.M. to 9:00 P.M. by Foster Burns and Baxter Ireland, the first two air traffic "cops" hired, working seven-hour shifts. The men used a two-way radio to communicate with those planes that had radios, and a portable red-light, green-light traffic, or "biscuit," gun for those that did not. The gun's light could be seen for 10 miles during the day and more than 20 miles at night. The matchbox contained loudspeakers that picked up radio traffic on all wave lengths to monitor where every plane was at all times.

To complement the new control tower, a new radio beam that had been in the works for more than a year became operational at the end of March 1938. The radio beam broadcast from five, 130-foot towers erected in the shape of a cross north of the airport and functioned primarily as a homing device for incoming planes. Stretching south to Pueblo, north to Cheyenne, east to Cozard, Nebraska, and west to the Moffit Tunnel, the beam formed a straight airway from these points to the municipal airport. When a pilot was directly on the airway, he could hear in his earphones a long dash signal. If he was to the right of the airway, he would hear a dash-dot code, and if he was to the left he would hear a dot-dash signal.

The radio beam station was operated by the CAA by remote control from an office at the airport. The signal could be changed any time from its landing code to voice transmission by simply dialing a code on the telephone. Periodically, the beam would transmit weather conditions, wind velocity and direction for every 1,000 feet of altitude up to 20,000 feet, and airport conditions of other fields as far away as Chicago, Salt Lake City, Billings and El Paso. The only other airport to have such a facility at the time was at Hartford, Connecticut.

The entire lighting system for Denver Municipal was revamped in 1938, with 36 new lights added to bring the total number to 106 that surrounded the field and runways. The lights were mounted on cones and the wires that ran to them were buried a few inches into the ground. Also in 1938, the airport installed a searchlight-type device near Ulster Street that could accurately tell the ceiling of clouds.

Once again in 1938, because of technological advances and improvements at the airport, the CAA gave Denver Municipal a top rating.

With all the activity going on at the airport, the 1938 Air Show drew a large crowd. It was a one-day affair, staged Sunday, September 18, again sponsored by the National Aeronautic Association and the Denver Chamber of Commerce. A parade of 40 planes flew over Denver to start the show.

More than 60,000 came out to see formation flying by the Colorado National Guard, the Pants Off race, precision flying, aerial stunts and parachutists. There was a small "cub" plane that supposedly got away from its handlers while it was being taxied around the apron area and the announcer, according to the *Rocky Mountain News,* September 19, called through the PA system: "There's only a little girl in the plane. Call the ambulance." In actuality, the "little girl" was a woman flyer in bloomers. There was also a bombing contest where flyers dropped sacks of flour on a circle drawn on a runway, reflecting the growing threat of world war.

The mood of the event, however, was festive, and a *Rocky Mountain News* reporter joined in the fun: "Throughout the afternoon the loudspeakers advertised for children lost in the crowd. Wives also put in requests that the announcer attempt to locate missing husbands. Husbands did not seem to have the same trouble."

In early 1939, Denver citizens took another initiative to promote Denver and its airport as a regional air hub with national importance. A delegation from the city, headed by Captain Ray Wilson of the Colorado National Guard, went to Washington in February to present a specific four-point proposal to a forum being sponsored by the new CAA. The first point called for designating the University of Colorado in Boulder and Denver as an instruction center for student pilots under the $10 million CAA instruction program already in progress.

Point two recommended the use of Denver civilian flying schools for flight training of military personnel under the pending National Defense Bill. President Franklin Roosevelt, through his defense bill and other legislation, was calling for a build up of U.S. defenses, including substantial boosting of the Army Air Corps. The corps, Roosevelt knew, did not have enough trained pilots, but there were not enough military flight schools to increase their numbers significantly. So, in the pending National Defense Bill there was a section that stated civilian flight training schools could be taken over or used to train military personnel, with the government reimbursing the schools for their time.

Denver wanted to house some of these government-sponsored schools.

Point three of the Denver delegation's proposal called for pressure to be put on some airplane manufacturers to relocate in Denver. The final point was for the establishment of airmail feeder routes to be run from Denver to Western Slope cities.

These four points, Denver politicians and aviation experts felt, would bring about new national awareness of Denver as an important aviation center. And that was just what most people in Denver wanted then.

While the delegation was still in Washington, construction and improvement plans were once again announced for the airport. A series of WPA projects would begin immediately to upgrade Denver Municipal. A new diagonal runway from the northeast to the southwest would be constructed with a rock base and oil surface and would be 6,000 feet long and 500 feet wide. The north-south runway would be reconditioned and taxiways from all runway extremities to the hangars would be built.

But these plans were abruptly halted by the CAA when it was discovered that Denver Municipal's asphalt runways were having trouble. In May of 1939, George E. Cranmer was called to Washington to explain to the CAA why Denver Municipal's runways were buckling. The asphalt that had been put down on the runways in 1937 and 1938 had begun to buckle after the first winter cold had hit them. Also, drainage of the two runways had not been properly designed, so that by the time Cranmer was called to Washington, 1,200 feet of the north-south and 800 feet of the east-west were useless. The problem had become so bad that some of the larger aircraft used by United Airlines and the Army had actually had their wheels sink into the asphalt while warming up for takeoff.

When the full extent of the problem was discovered by the CAA, it called an immediate halt to all large aircraft landing at Denver Municipal and an immediate halt to the construction being done on the new diagonal runway. Within a few months, however, all runways had been repaired, the CAA revoked its ban on large aircraft and construction was continued on the diagonal runway.

*In an effort to upgrade the technological aspects of flying, the CAA (Civil Aeronautic Association) erected five towers north of the airport that emitted homing beams in four directions for in-flying planes. Courtesy of the* Denver Post.

*The CAA's homing beams could also voice broadcast. Transmission was controlled from Denver Municipal by CAA superintendent William A. Breniman. Courtesy of the* Denver Post.

*In the late 1930s weather balloons were sent up every six hours, day and night, to test weather conditions. Courtesy of the* Denver Post.

On September 18, 1938, 60,000 people came to Denver Municipal for the free airshow. A parade of 40 planes flew over Denver to start the show. Courtesy of the Denver Post.

On August 22, 1938, Denverites came to look at a new type of bomber, the B-17, or flying fortress. Later, during World War II, bombers like the one shown here, would become famous for their bombing runs over Europe (opposite, above). Courtesy of the Denver Post.

By 1939 Denver Municipal boasted three hangars and a control tower (opposite, below). Courtesy of the Western History Department, Denver Public Library.

Nine Army attack planes stayed over night at Denver Municipal on October 16, 1938, on their way to California. Courtesy of the Denver Post.

*Bomb instruction. Courtesy of the Western History Department, Denver Public Library.*

# Chapter Three

As the world exploded into 1940, President Franklin Roosevelt continued to build U.S. defenses via the National Defense Bill while maintaining that the United States would stay out of the war. But soon he was backing lend-lease to England and calling for the United States to become the "arsenal of democracy." With Hitler's blitzkrieg, which utilized airplanes as never before, and Japan's dependence upon aircraft in its fight against China, Roosevelt realized that the United States would need a strong air defense and air force when the country entered the war.

What this meant to Americans was new jobs and revenues generated by the government's proposed air bases and manufacturing plants. A city that could attract government installations and personnel would be guaranteed income from government contracts, which could mean the difference between local prosperity or continued depression.

Denver was no different than any other city around the country—it desperately wanted to attract federal monies through government defense programs. Many in the city believed the best way to do this was through the promotion of Denver as an aviation center. This promotion could have the added benefit of drawing more commercial airline companies to the area. Realizing that aviation growth would mean a more stable local economy, Denver's citizens and newspapers began a concerted effort to promote the area and its aviation facilities.

The *Rocky Mountain News*, in the early 1940s, began using a logo at the corner of each aviation-related article as part of its promotion drive. The logo featured a sketch of a small mono-winged, single-engine plane in flight with the mountains as a backdrop and with the words "Make Denver a National Air Center." Any aviation news made big headlines: composite stories and editorials called for this or that to be done to get Denver on the national aviation map. A *Rocky Mountain News* story about Lowry Field, run on July 2, 1940, reflected this constant promotion. Part of the article stated, "It is particularly pertinent to state that the all-year-round climate and the availability of a varied terrain were very influential in originally placing the school [Lowry] here, and have continued to play a very important part in

the tremendous improvements and increases that have been in progress since its inception."

With such a drive going on, the city began to receive aviation recognition. On July 8, 1940, the National Aeronautic Association came to Denver to hold the National Air Conference. This was the first time the prestigious conference was held in Denver. Also, the government decided to build Buckley Air Base in Colorado, which was commissioned in 1941 and used as an auxiliary field to Lowry. It was located east of Lowry and southwest of Denver Municipal, between Colfax Avenue and Mississippi, and Chambers Road and the boundary line of Denver and Adams counties. (Buckley was deactivated at the end of the war and was reactivated by the U.S. Navy in February 1947.)

## Denver Municipal Enters the 1940s

Denver Municipal Airport was the keystone of Denver's attempt at attracting both federal and commercial airline business. Because of this, the 1940s ushered in a new era for the airport. During Denver Municipal's first 11 years, many people viewed it as more of a novelty than as a business that could help the city grow. But the 1940s changed that as Denver Municipal developed into a major business with all the corresponding problems and rewards.

Although the 1940s were important because of the expansion and growth that took place at the airport, they were also important because they foreshadowed the problems and situations the airport would face during the next three decades. Such present-day concerns like master plans, citizen protests, and Rocky Mountain Arsenal land battles all had their roots in the 1940s.

The tremendous increase in air travel and operations in the 1940s, due primarily to the war, forced city and Denver Municipal officials into planning construction and improvements years in advance. This long-range planning began taking the name "master plan" and, from the late 1940s on, Denver Municipal's history reveals some type of master plan constantly being developed, revised, implemented or just completed. And, with long-range planning came airport consultants

*During the early 1940s the news media supported the concept of expanding Denver's importance in aviation. The* Rocky Mountain News *placed the above logo at the beginning of every aviation-oriented article. Excerpt from the* Rocky Mountain News, *courtesy of the Colorado Historical Society.*

—outside experts hired by the city to project growth and suggest measures to handle the demands of that future growth.

As construction and improvements were called for in the 1940s, the airport also had to grow in acreage. Although some small parcels of land had been acquired in the 1930s, the land acquisition begun in the 1940s heralded the start of aggressive airport land expansion that would only cease in the 1960s. With this policy, however, came citizen protests, for residential and business communities had begun bordering the airport and did not want to give up any of their property.

Another change in the 1940s that would carry over into the future, was the method of financing airport growth. The airport construction and improvements in the 1930s had been paid for with money out of the city's general fund. But as construction and building costs increased, it became apparent in the 1940s that different funding arrangements had to be found. Self-liquidating bonds became the solution.

These bonds, which first appeared in the late 1940s, were used to build almost all of the airport that stands in the 1980s. They worked like this: A specific amount of proposed bonds—the estimated cost of construction—would be put before Denver voters for their approval. If the voters approved the bond issue, the bonds would be sold with the pay back coming from landing and rental fees and concession rentals by airport tenants. In this way, little or no money was used from Denver's general fund.

At the start, these bonds were primarily used to build facilities for the airlines—hangars and office buildings. However, throughout the next decades, the bonds were also used to expand the terminal and add runways to accommodate an ever increasing number of passengers and aircraft.

Complementing the bonds, through the years, was federal assistance. When it could be shown that construction was for the betterment of the general public, many times the government—through its aviation regulatory agencies—contributed half of the estimated costs.

The development in the 1940s that had the greatest future impact on the airport, however, was the establishment of the Rocky Mountain Arsenal. The Army bought the land from Adams County in June 1942 and by January 1943 it was an operational chemical warfare plant, adjoining Denver Municipal's north side. During the next three decades as the airport needed to expand, the Arsenal became the only feasible place to acquire land—the airport was hemmed in on all other sides by residential, business or county property. The Arsenal's large tract of mostly unoccupied land seemed ideal for Denver Municipal's needs. Unfortunately, Arsenal and Army officials did not always agree with that assessment. Throughout the rest of Denver Municipal's 50-year history, the airport had to constantly fight the Arsenal for parcels of land.

## The War Years at Denver Municipal

In 1940, improvements for Denver Municipal were announced as part of the national defense-building program. The plans included a new hangar (for United and Continental's administrative offices and planes), new lights for all runways, purchase of a snowplow, and drainage leveling of the runways and surrounding land. In addition, a new control tower, octagonal in shape, would replace the old "matchbox" tower atop the administration building. The new structure, 16 by 22 feet and enclosed by plate glass for 360 degrees visibility, would be air-conditioned and have a light on its roof for pilots to see during inclement weather. Construction of the tower, and the other projects, began in 1940 and were completed the following year.

Also in 1940, President Franklin Roosevelt approved a $110,000 appropriation to double the size of the Colorado National Guard hangar, built at Denver Municipal in 1937. Work was started in 1941 by 100 WPA workers, with Denver supplying the land. The north wall of the hangar was torn out for the enlargement, and a 30-car garage was added to the west side of the hangar.

Although the threat of war was on the minds of most Denver citizens in 1940, this did not stop the city from

*The airshow included stunt flyers, parachutists, and Colorado National Guard planes doing formation flying. Courtesy of the Western History Department, Denver Public Library.*

*A 1910 pusher type "buggy" plane was demonstrated at the airshow. Courtesy of the Western History Department, Denver Public Library.*

*During the Fourth of July weekend of 1940, the biggest crowd in Colorado's history (more than 100,000) gather for the Denver Municipal Airshow. Courtesy of the Western History Department, Denver Public Library.*

*By February 1941 a $300,000 WPA project hangar for United and Continental administrative offices had been started and the terminal building's third floor had been filled in. The pilot of the photo-taking plane was Charles Woodworth, airport manager. Courtesy of the* Denver Post.

*Classes in airplane nomenclature were held at Denver Municipal, Lowry and Buckley fields. Courtesy of the Western History Department, Denver Public Library.*

*The Colorado National Guard hangar took on new importance at Denver Municipal as the United States entered World War Two. During the war, the airport served as a repair base for bombers. Courtesy of the Colorado Historical Society.*

*Installation of machine guns aboard a fighter plane. Courtesy of the Western History Department, Denver Public Library.*

*During the war, Stapleton Airfield had a U.S.O. lounge where soldiers could relax before or between flights. Courtesy of the* Denver Post.

staging an air show at Denver Municipal Airport. It took place over the Fourth of July weekend and more than 100,000 people showed up for the first day's events. Some estimates had the crowd as large as 200,000. Whatever the figure, it was the biggest crowd to ever assemble in the state. For unknown reasons the event was called the First Annual Denver Air Show, though air shows had been taking place at Denver Municipal almost every year since 1929.

During the first day, a ground-breaking ceremony was held for the construction of the United/Continental $300,000 hangar. Mayor Stapleton turned over the ceremonial first shovelful of dirt, then announced to the crowd that the airport now ranked twelfth in the country in aircraft operations.

Also on the first day, University of Denver students conducted a study of the cars parked at the airport and discovered 31 of the 48 states were represented.

While the students were counting cars, the audience was being entertained by parachutists, stunt flyers, Colorado National Guard planes and a demonstration of an old 1910 pusher type "buggy" plane. There was also a performance by a flyer, supposedly drunk, who staged aerial stunts at low-level.

The two-day event ended with a banquet and ball at the Brown Palace Hotel, attended by city, state and military officials, as well as flyers who had participated in the show.

By 1941, the new control tower was operational and all other construction that had been announced in 1940 was completed. Because of these improvements, the CAA gave the airport its highest rating, a "4."

In early 1941, the CAA announced that its offices at Denver Municipal would be enlarged. Part of this expansion included a teletype center to compile aviation information and weather conditions from all teletype lines across the country. The CAA's teletype center was one of only two such centers in the country—the other was located in Louisville, Kentucky. With the new system, the CAA could better assist and control aerial activity throughout the Rocky Mountain states. As part of the expansion plan, the CAA took over all of the second floor of the administration building and part of the third floor. United and Continental, who occupied those spaces, moved to their newly built hangar facilities.

After the attack on Pearl Harbor, December 7, 1941, and subsequent declarations of war by Germany and Italy on the United States, Americans learned, once again, about wartime situations. The government became extremely secretive about anything to do with national defense. Complying with the government's wishes for secrecy, the majority of newspapers refrained from reporting on any topic deemed to be of a wartime or defensive nature.

In Denver, during the bleak days of 1942 when U.S. forces were being badly beaten in the Pacific, little was mentioned of Lowry, Buckley, or Denver Municipal airports. One of the few items that did get in the papers in 1942 concerned land acquisition for future lengthening of Denver Municipal's east-west runway. The runway would be extended to almost 10,000 feet in order to handle the heaviest of U.S. bombers, which needed longer runways than commercial planes. The land needed for this extension was 160 acres east of the airport and was acquired from private citizens as well as an organization called the Clayton Trust. The runway, however, was not extended until 1948, and then it was only lengthened to 8,500 feet.

When the war had broken out, commercial air carriers had been pressed into government service. Their planes were used to fly military personnel and cargo all across the country, and military pilots were trained by many of these commercial carriers. Another government utilization of these airlines was in modifying the larger commercial aircraft into bombers. For the first few years of the war, Continental—as part of this program—used the Colorado National Guard hangar at Denver Municipal to modify aircraft, which had been built on the West Coast.

As the demands for modification increased, however, the government became more directly involved, building a modification center near Denver Municipal in early 1943. This "little known to the public" center, according to the *Denver Post*, July 18, 1943, was the largest construction job in Denver's history. It was located on 90 acres near the airport, and the main building was 600 by 480 feet—more than four times the size of the Denver Municipal's original 1929 hangar. The center was declared surplus after the war, and on December 1, 1945, it was officially turned over to Denver, which incorporated it into Denver Municipal and rented it out to the airline companies.

## 1943—Denver Turns to the Future

"It is my belief that the postwar prosperity and welfare of Denver are more peculiarly bound up with the progress of air commerce than those of almost any other major United States city." This statement from Brigadier General Harvey S. Burnwell, former commandant of Lowry Field, was part of an editorial series run by the *Denver Post* in July 1943, about air power in the postwar years and how it pertained to Denver. The writer was Elvon L. Howe.

The whole article was indicative of how the war was progressing. On all fronts the United States and its Allies

were winning, and newspaper space was equally divided between battle campaigns and forecasts of the postwar era. In Denver, newspaper coverage of these forecasts included a great deal on aviation. As the *Denver Post* article stated, "In the most immediate and definite future, airline men with hardly any exception now concede that Denver will inevitably be the hub of domestic air commerce for the whole west."

As evidence for this statement, Howe noted there were two government airfields in Denver (Lowry and Buckley) and the CAA had an air traffic control center at Denver Municipal which governed airways in several states. In addition, Howe mentioned, on May 1, 1943, three new air routes in and out of Denver Municipal had been approved by the CAB, with three more up for consideration. The three approved routes were Continental's Denver–Kansas City, United's Denver–Washington, D.C., and Braniff's Denver–Amarillo. Howe also reported that Mayor Stapleton, still aviation conscious, had vowed to make "the city's aviation progress one of the major administration efforts in his present term."

The *Denver Post* felt that postwar aviation in Denver was important enough to give the article an entire page, and included an air-route map of the world with Denver as its hub. Air-route lines on the map radiated out from the city to all parts of the world. Part of Howe's conclusion was that, "One thing is certain. If Denver is to be an air center, it must become thoroughly air minded, and not gradually, but quickly. It's an air world."

Howe also wrote: "If it can be assumed that immediately after war, hundreds of thousands of citizens will take to the air in trim, safe, comfortable little family airplanes on errands of business, shopping, or merely visiting, then the segregation of light airplanes from bigger and faster airliners and freighters is an absolute necessity."

What Howe was referring to was general aviation aircraft at Denver's airport. As commercial aircraft operations increased at Denver Municipal, so did general aviation operations. Although the smaller private planes did not experience great growth until after the war, all through Denver Municipal's history general aviation had been increasing. And with this increase came congestion of the airways and runways at the airport.

Many major airports around the country had experienced similar congestion through the 1930s and 1940s. Most of these airports had solved the problem by banning private aircraft from their facilities. General aviation had simply moved to local, smaller airports that catered to them or had the government help build those types of facilities.

Mayor Stapleton decided in May of 1943 to solve Denver Municipal's growing problem of congestion by

*With the world at war, a national holiday came to symbolize military strength. Here 260 parachutists from the 507th Parachutist Infantry Regiment land at Denver Municipal Airport on July 4, 1943. Courtesy of the* Denver Post.

*In 1941 the CAA, which controlled a five-state area, expanded its traffic control offices at the airport, taking over the complete second floor and part of the third floor. This picture, taken in August 1942, was the first published picture of the traffic control center. Courtesy of the* Denver Post.

relocating general aviation. His proposal called for the purchase of 2,000 acres south of the city, in Arapahoe County, where a small-plane airport could be built.

This project met the same, if not more, resistance than "Stapleton's Folly" had back in the late 1920s. The resistance this time came from the farmers of Arapahoe County, who believed conversion of the land from agriculture to aviation use would rob valuable farmland from the war effort.

The battle between Denver politicians and Arapahoe County farmers raged throughout 1943, until in January 1944, a judge placed a court injunction on the project.

In November 1945, the project resurfaced in the news when Denver bought a parcel of 320 acres in Arapahoe County for the proposed airport. This parcel was added to a 160-acre parcel purchased back in 1943.

Arapahoe County farmers, though, would not give in, taking their case to court again and blocking the project. A final resolution was not reached, however, until September 1958, when Denver, realizing it had lost the battle, sold off the 480 acres it had purchased. The city had bought the land for $80,000 and sold it for $1,164,800. The former owners of the land received $676,000 to compensate for the increased value of the land.

With the failure of this project, small aircraft remained at the Denver Municipal Airport. But with military, commercial and general aviation using Denver Municipal, Lowry and Buckley fields, it was only a matter of time before the law of averages caught up with the area and the first major air crash occurred.

On September 27, 1943, at 9:30 A.M., a routine training flight of a Liberator B-24 bomber out of Lowry Field suddenly lost control and dropped from the skies. The plane crashed in a vacant lot in the 2500 block of South Marion Street, a block from the Sanatorium. As reported in the *Rocky Mountain News*, September 27, 1943, all seven crew members were killed and three houses were set ablaze by the "streets of flames that burst in all directions from the ship." No reason was given for the crash, but eye witnesses agreed that the pilot looked as if he had fought to bring the plane down in a vacant lot rather than crash into the rows of houses nearby.

Another crash of a Liberator bomber in the Colorado Springs area only 48 hours later, brought a great outcry from those residents living near airports. Their demands for tighter and better control of civilian, commercial and military planes flying around Denver reflected a growing national concern for air safety.

As a result of this public protest, an Army Flight Control Center was established at Denver Municipal in early 1944. The Army planned to use the CAA's communication facilities (which revolved around the teletype center and the radio beam), to plot every Army

flight while in the air. The control center would check and recheck how each flight was proceeding throughout the entire area. While checking on flights, the control center would also transmit weather conditions and field conditions to the airborne planes. This Denver Army center was one of 23 such centers established throughout the country.

Denver Municipal also helped air safety by clearing the northern approach to the airport in early 1944. The houses and storage buildings which blocked this approach were razed to relieve the congestion of smaller buildings at the airport. This was done as part of a program to make the airport more accessible to airplanes in all directions.

## Denver Municipal Gets a New Name

Ben Stapleton, who was nearing the end of his long political career by 1944, had done more to promote and expand the airport than any other single individual. This was, obviously, due in part to the fact that it was the airport he had envisioned in the early 1920s and had helped to build. But it was also due in part to the overall commitment Stapleton had made to help Denver grow and change with the times. Denver Municipal Airport, Stapleton knew from the beginning, was a key ingredient to national aviation recognition, both directly and indirectly.

The airport had been partially responsible for the establishment of Lowry air base, and directly responsible for hundreds of jobs and much-needed revenues that came to the city through WPA projects and federal funds used to expand Denver Municipal. Stapleton's initial foresight and continued understanding of the needs of the airport—and what it could ultimately do for the city—kept the facility abreast of the rapidly changing aviation industry.

In 1944, the city finally gave Stapleton the full recognition he deserved for making the airport one of the best and most used aerial facilities in the country. The city declared that on August 25, 1944, Denver Municipal Airport would become Stapleton Airfield. Stapleton was honored at a dinner staged by Continental, United and Western airlines at the Brown Palace Hotel, with the ceremonies held at the airport on August 25. The renaming of the facility coincided with the presentation of the National Safety Award—for "superior protection of personnel and facilities"—to Mayor Stapleton by Brigadier General Albert L. Sneed, commander of Lowry. The radio station, KOA, broadcast both events, which attracted state, local and federal officials, military personnel and the Buckley Field band.

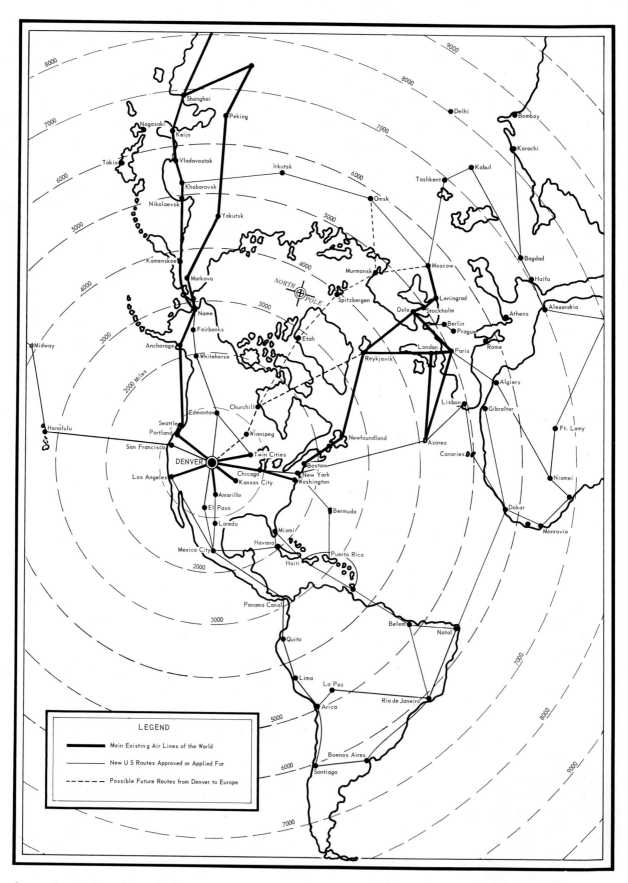

*In a major article on Denver's place in post war aviation, the* Denver Post *ran this world map showing Denver as the hub to show how the Mile High city was connected by air to the whole world. Courtesy of the* Denver Post.

*By the early 1940s general aviation aircraft were creating congestion problems for the growing airport. But the revenues generated by the planes saved them from being evicted from Denver Municipal. Courtesy of the* Denver Post.

*On August 25, 1944, Denver Municipal Airport had its name officially changed to Stapleton Airfield in honor of Mayor Ben Stapleton. The Color Guard displayed the new pennant for the airport. Courtesy of the University of Denver.*

## Postwar Activity

By 1945, Stapleton Airfield appeared to be growing into the air hub Denver had hoped for. Its original 640 acres had increased to 1,435, there were four runways (one east-west, one north-south and two diagonals) and 40–50 commercial flights a day. The airport employed more than 1,200 people and had two flying schools and four major airlines operating from its facilities. The original administration building was still standing, along with six hangars, an airport Post Office, a fire station, a traffic control tower, a U.S.O. lounge and a cafe. Stapleton also housed the CAA's five-state airway traffic control, staffed with 35 CAA personnel and 10 Army flight control men who coordinated commercial, private and military flights.

But this growth did not stop local politicians and airport officials from anticipating further growth and developing plans to meet it. In September 1945, George Cranmer announced a proposed plan for building a new terminal. The structure would be in a horseshoe shape made up of terminal "units" two stories high and 130 feet long. It would be 1,200–1,400 feet long with 850 feet of space between the ends of the horseshoe. Cranmer told the *Rocky Mountain News* on September 15, 1945, that the "principal advantage claimed over the old style terminals is that passengers at the airport can get to their planes after only a short walk even if departures in the future are doubled or trebled."

Cranmer also said that he and Mayor Stapleton had been developing the plan for the past three years. They had visited Chicago's O'Hare Airport for ideas and thought the horseshoe shape would work well because it could be expanded as much as a quarter mile if future demand called for it. In early 1946, Mayor Stapleton was meeting periodically with his airport committee to discuss the expansion plans. By this time, the plan also called for a new control tower and a large restaurant within the terminal.

After numerous discussions and debates with politicians and airport officials, it was also agreed that the east-west runway should be expanded. (This was originally discussed in 1942.) The plan called for the runway to be lengthened to 10,000 feet; but that, however, was cut back so that when it was completed in 1948, the runway was only 8,500.

With talk of Mayor Stapleton's multimillion-dollar master plan, airport safety measures again became an issue. The *Rocky Mountain News* ran a story on August 18, 1946, about the fire-fighting ability—or lack of ability—at Stapleton Airfield. Engine Company #22 was responsible for the entire airport yet had only eight men—four on a shift—and two fire trucks. Each truck had a capacity of 850 gallons of water when not hooked up to a hydrant. This meant that if both trucks responded to an air crash not near a hydrant (most of the runways were near hydrants), they would be out of water in a matter of minutes, with only chemical agents left to retard the blaze.

The *News* reported that during World War II the Army had been responsible for airport fire fighting and had used 32 men, 11 on duty at a time—this was four times the men at the airport in 1946. When questioned about the number of peacetime firemen, the fire company responded by stating there were not enough city funds to support additional personnel. It was mentioned by the fire department, however, that the Stapleton station was hooked up to the downtown station so more fire trucks could be called if necessary. The problem with that, of course, was that by the time fire trucks could respond from downtown, many lives could be lost in an aircraft blaze.

Although during the next few years another truck and more men were added to the Stapleton fire station, it would take a major air crash at the airport in the early 1960s before significant changes were made in Stapleton Airfield's fire-fighting capacity.

On the lighter side of 1946, Stapleton Airfield held its first postwar air show, the Denver International Air Show, on August 24 and 25. With the war over, participants included famous military flying teams that had been formed during the war. The Blue Angels, a Navy stunt team, participated in their F7F aircraft and, as the commander of the Angels said, could use heretofore secret aerial tactics in their stunts. Four Marine Aces, called the Tiger Cats, also flew in the show. And a special appearance was made by the Army's experimental Northrup Flying Wing fighter plane that had reached a speed of more than 720 miles per hour.

Although the event was not scheduled to begin until August 24, on August 23 the military pilots staged a dress rehearsal for the wounded at Fitzsimmons General Hospital. This preview show had an interesting highlight when Harvey, the six-foot rabbit from the Broadway play, made himself visible to the wounded at the hospital. He had flown in from New York City especially for the preview.

Twenty thousand people attended the official opening day of the air show. The newspapers reported that the Blue Angels were the best of the aerial entertainment, maneuvering their planes at 400 miles per hour as if piloted by one person, and staging a mock dogfight with a Japanese Zero which supposedly went down in flames. The last act of the show was a mass takeoff by all the Army planes including Mustangs, Flying Fortresses, Super Fortresses, Thunderbolts, Lightnings, P-80s, Black Widows and even a jet-propelled Shooting Star.

On the second—and final—day of the show, more than 50,000 people turned out to see the aerial acrobatics. Rain temporarily delayed the show for an hour and a half but did not deter the spectators, who stayed to watch the events.

## Postwar Optimism About Aviation Growth Dies

A sad note to 1946 was that it was the last year Ben Stapleton served Denver as mayor. He left office after finalizing the master plan, which had grown to an estimated cost of $3.5 million. No construction had begun on Stapleton Airfield, though, because the plan needed approval from the CAA and financial aid from the federal government. But Denver was ready to back the plan and finance its half through the city's general fund and bond issues.

Unfortunately, Denver's new mayor, Quigg Newton, quickly put a stop to the whole plan. The city had already paid out $55,000 to have the plan drawn up, but Mayor Newton felt the whole concept was too ambitious for the present-day activity at the airport. He told the *Rocky Mountain News* on August 17, 1947: "It's merely the wartime optimism about the future of air travel hasn't quite panned out. Now we have to seek more moderate ideas. We will, however, begin preparation of a set of plans on a more moderate scale."

Mayor Newton did, however, authorize $250,000 for emergency repair work on runways and other facilities showing signs of wear. These repairs were a necessity, for the CAA had reviewed Stapleton Airfield a short time before and had threatened to shut down the airport due to unsafe conditions. The emergency work included ripping up and resurfacing 1,800 feet of the north-south runway and 50–100 feet of the east-west runway, repairs to the apron in front of the administration building, installation of a storm sewer, reboring and resurfacing of the warm-up pad on the east-west runway and adjustment of all runway lights. The work was started immediately and finished by November 1947.

With Mayor Newton's rejection of Stapleton's $3.5 million expansion program, many thought Stapleton Airfield would decline in national ranking. On August 28, 1947, the *Denver Post* ran a front-page banner headline story about the airport. Stapleton Airfield, the article reported, served all types of aircraft— from Army, Navy and Air Force planes to private and commercial craft—while many large airports had already limited their service to commercial planes; leaving private pilots to land at smaller, less-congested fields and military pilots to land at government-owned fields. Six major airlines were stationed at Stapleton (Continental, United, Western, Monarch, Challenger and Braniff) and, from figures gathered by these companies, 200,750 passengers annually boarded or deplaned on the 75 commercial flights per day. The peak period was from 1:00 P.M. to

2:00 P.M., when 175 passengers arrived or departed.

The article mentioned that in 1936 the facility ranked with the best airports in the country, but now ranked only eighth nationally in total operations. "Denver's enviable position among terminal cities is sliding as if on greased skids. One of the few major cities handling both northbound, southbound, eastbound and westbound traffic, Stapleton Airport may be by-passed unless it meets the challenge offered by other major cities."

The article went on to report that, "airline officials now classify Denver's air facilities in the lowest bracket and from 'mediocre' to the 'poorest service in the country.'"

Major criticism, the article related, revolved around Stapleton's runways: They were too weak and short for the larger, heavier types of commercial craft entering service across the country. And this problem could have extreme consequences: "This shortcoming alone [too short and weak runways] may be the deciding factor in Stapleton's future as a mainline or a whistle stop."

But the runways were not the only problem, the *Post* reported: "Stapleton airport, experts agree, is weak in every aspect. Comfort of passengers, a prime requisite, is practically forgotten here. Accommodations of every nature must be sought from sources other than the terminal building."

The article did state that the city, as part of a revised plan on the original $3.5 million plan, would be spending $2 million in 1947 and 1948, but only to "restore and make permanent the bare essentials of an airport." The *Post* believed that this was not enough, citing other cities—specifically San Francisco, Milwaukee, Los Angeles, Boston, Toledo, Newark, Washington, D.C., Pittsburgh and Chicago—whose appropriations were $4 million to $75 million for "anticipating the future."

The article warned, "Denver's Stapleton Airport is stirring from its 18-year lethargy—but its eyes will have to be wide open soon to maintain its secure position among alert, municipally owned fields."

(This last statement was a somewhat unfair evaluation of the airport's 18-year history. The facility had definitely not remained lethargic, rather it had grown and changed as rapidly as Denver could afford it, meeting the needs of a new and constantly changing transportation industry. It was easy in hindsight to criticize the actions of city and airport officials since the airport's beginnings in 1929, but aviation's phenomenal growth from 1929 to 1947 had been impossible to predict.)

With Denver newspapers, local politicians and airport officials calling for more, rather than less, improvements, Mayor Newton decided in September 1947 to form a committee to study the airport and propose ways

*The new terminal was needed because of the congestion that plagued the airport in the 1940s. Courtesy of the* Denver Post.

*Although only 15 to 20 years had gone by since its founding, Stapleton Airfield had a different look to it. Courtesy of Stapleton International Airport.*

By 1945 the airport's original 640 acres had increased to 1,435, there were four runways and 40-50 commercial flights a day. In September, George Cranmer presented a plan for a new horseshoe-shaped terminal made up of "units," that were two stories and 130 feet long. The plan was rejected but the airport would ultimately take on the horseshoe shape. Courtesy of the Denver Post.

Although only 15 to 20 years had gone by since its founding, Stapleton Airfield had a different look to it. Courtesy of Stapleton International Airport.

of making it the best in the country. He was still determined to keep the costs in line, but he realized that a total rejection of major improvements at Stapleton could have serious consequences for Denver's future aviation standing.

Mayor Newton's committee was composed of airline officials, aviation experts and military personnel, so that all viewpoints would be represented. Although their complete master plan for the future would not be ready until 1948, the committee immediately proposed a three-point plan for emergency improvements. The north-south runway, the committee said, should be repaired and resurfaced, the parking spaces in hangars one and two should be cleared, and a construction program should be begun to provide office and passenger space for the airlines that were located in the World War II Quonset huts south of the administration building. These actions were approved by the city and work was started immediately.

The committee also reviewed a proposal from United Airlines, which was moving its operations base to Stapleton in 1948 and needed 80,000 square feet to house its new headquarters. United asked the city to build its office, with construction costs being amortized over a long rental period. The mayor's committee was to look into the possibility of financing the project through a bond issue.

Because United's move to Denver was seen as good for business, a group of Denver businessmen, led by Claude K. Boettcher, agreed to underwrite any proposed bond issue. (Although the idea was quickly agreed to in principle, it would not be until 1953 that United had its office building.)

During the fall of 1947, discussion centered around the question of how the city would pay for any improvements, and whether or not the airfield was worth the money. In November, a report by Mayor Newton and director of aviation, John Curry, was released to the public. The report stated, "While the Airport may show a financial deficit for the next few years, due to the large capital expenditures entailed in the reconstruction of the flying field and the terminal area, Stapleton Airfield itself is a great economic asset to the city."

To back up this claim, the report cited the fact that the commercial and private airlines employed 1,750 people

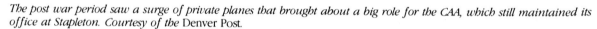

*The post war period saw a surge of private planes that brought about a big role for the CAA, which still maintained its office at Stapleton. Courtesy of the* Denver Post.

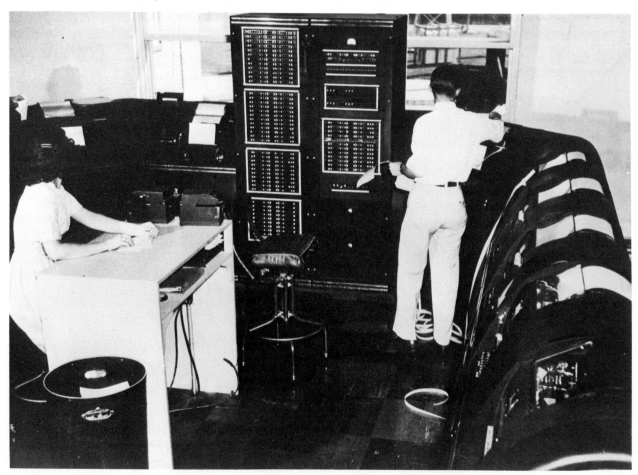

at the airport, and city taxes levied on the airlines amounted to $50,000 a year. Curry, reported the *Rocky Mountain News* on November 22, said:

> The Airport really is in the status of any of your public works which are necessary to serve the people of the city and to enable it to grow.
>
> Even if Stapleton Airfield gave no direct financial return it would, like other modern improvements, be a most worthwhile civic enterprise. It does, however, give a financial return even though that may not cover all its expenses, and it is a vital part of a progressive city.

The report also stated that since 1940, Stapleton Airfield had moved from thirty-second to nineteenth place in the number of passengers using the airport, and from twenty-third to fifteenth in the number of airline passenger miles flown. Ticket sales had also increased during this time from 2,439 to 26,146—almost an elevenfold increase in only seven years.

Because of such growth, the CAA in 1947 included Stapleton Airfield in the 32 airports across the country that would receive equipment for a new landing technique called "Instrument Landing System" (ILS). The ILS worked by using specialized radio receivers installed in airplane cockpits, which received directional radio beams from local units at an airport. There were two types of beams, one for a directional approach to the airport and one for the plane's angle of descent. In the newspaper article announcing the ILS, there was also a mention of a newer system that might soon make the ILS obsolete. This experimental system was the "Very High Frequency" radio, or VHF, that was then in the developmental stage.

Another important development that was begun in 1947 was the move to change Denver's charter. The city had had the same governmental organization and charter for 43 years and many felt it was time for a change. Charter delegates met in the summer of 1947 to develop a new organization plan. Stapleton was only affected by this move through the reorganization of its regulatory agency. For its 18-year life span, Stapleton Airfield had been under the jurisdiction of the Department of Parks and Improvements. Under the proposed new charter, that department would be split into the Parks and Recreation Division and the Public Works Division. The airport would be under the jurisdiction of the Public Works Division. The proposed Charter was never passed, but in May 1955, an amendment was passed that broke up the parks department into the two separate divisions.

Another interesting event that took place in 1947 was the move in October to take bids from farmers on growing winter wheat on the vacant 1,240 acres in and around Stapleton Airfield. The city had to cut and burn off the weeds that grew on this acreage every spring, and it was felt that the land could be better utilized. The farmer that won the contract would work on a sharecropper basis. Most of the land that would be planted was bounded by Montview Boulevard, East Forty-second Street, Havana and Syracuse.

## Mayor Newton's Master Plan is Finalized—Work is Begun

By the beginning of 1948, Mayor Newton's master plan for Stapleton expansion was finalized. It would include the building of two major runways (one east-west and one north-south) and substantial additions to the terminal building.

Mayor Newton's runways proposal involved a new 7,500-foot north-south runway that would cost $630,000 as well as a new 8,500-foot east-west runway costing $911,000. The north-south runway would be built in 1949, and the east-west in 1948. The airport had spent $367,789 on runway maintenance during the last five years, and many thought it would be cheaper in the long run to build these two new runways than to constantly spend money on repairing the old ones.

For the proposed runways, Stapleton Airfield would once again have to be enlarged. In April 1948, an agreement was reached between Denver and Aurora to buy an eight-block area in the northwest corner of Aurora. This parcel was between Boston and Dayton streets, and East Twenty-fifth and East Twenty-sixth avenues.

Also in April, Denver's expansion plan for Stapleton received a windfall. The CAB announced it would help finance the east-west runway. Because of this windfall, it was decided to use the city money that had been earmarked for the east-west runway to better improve the terminal facilities. It was also decided that with the improved terminal facilities and east-west runway, the north-south runway plans would be cancelled. The 8,500-foot asphalt east-west runway was completed in November, having been built south of the old east-west runway.

The terminal improvements called for in Mayor Newton's master plan did not include the horseshoe-shaped terminal of Mayor Stapleton's plan. Newton's plan was for two wings, two stories high, to be added to the north and south ends of the old three-story terminal building (still the original structure built in 1929). The new terminal wings would be of red flagstone and the present terminal would be remodeled to blend in with it. On the first floor of the expanded terminal, there would be a snack bar, open all hours; a barber shop, a beauty parlor; and other concessions. The additions would allow 50 percent more lobby space to handle the increasing number of passengers flying in 1948. There

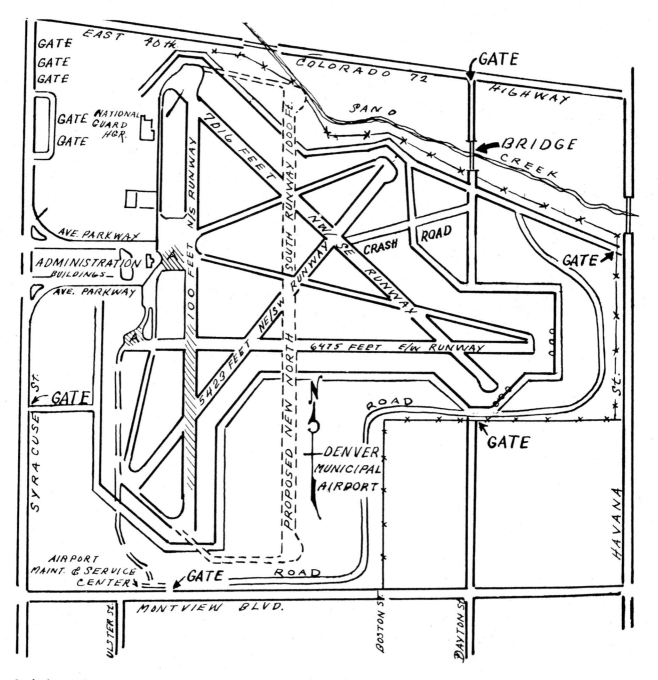

*In the late 1940s a new north-south runway was proposed, but was ultimately cancelled and an east-west runway was built instead. Courtesy of the* Denver Post.

would also be more airline ticket counter and baggage claim space for the six major airlines.

The second story of the south wing of the new terminal would house a huge restaurant, able to seat 230 people, and a cocktail lounge. The restaurant and lounge would be glass-enclosed on the east, south and west sides so people could watch the planes and see the mountains while dining or drinking. Charles J. Lowen, aviation director of Stapleton, told the *Denver Post* on September 23, 1948, "We believe that the dining room will become one of the most popular eating places in Denver."

The control tower, atop the old terminal structure would remain there for the present time, for its facilities were believed adequate for the airport's needs.

With the proposed additions to the north and south of the old terminal, hangar number one (the original hangar of the 1929 airport), which was just north of the terminal, would be moved. The hangar would go to the western edge of the airfield, north of the modification center, and that whole area of the field would be used for private, small planes. The buildings south of the terminal would be razed so that the south wing could be built. These buildings were the cafe (originally, in 1929, the fire house), airline freight offices, and the Quonset huts built during World War II.

Although work was begun immediately on the runway part of Mayor Newton's plan, terminal construction would have to wait until bids were taken on the work. By November of 1948, bids were in for both north and south wings. The bids on the north terminal wing were found to be so much higher than the original estimates that Newton decided to cancel construction of the north wing and only build the south wing. The restaurant and lounge would not be affected by the decision because they were both located in the south wing, but the lobby space, ticket counters and airline office space would be cut. Construction of the south wing was begun in early 1949.

Mayor Newton's master plan was primarily developed to improve the airport facilities and relieve the congestion of both passengers and planes. But some aviation people felt the plan was not enough. In 1948, a proposal was made in aviation circles to completely reorganize Stapleton Airfield. This proposal called for commercial flights to be diverted to Lowry and Stapleton Airfield to be leased to private, reserve and National Guard planes. The proposal also called for the building of a 10,000-foot north-south runway east of Lowry to be connected with Lowry's southwest and east-west runways. The city would hold title to the 10,000-foot runway and build facilities around it. The *Denver Post*, on April 11, quoted proponents of the proposal as saying, "You can never make a first-class airport out of Stapleton Field because it is hemmed in on the north and south, where 75 percent of the landings and takeoffs are made."

Another point of view on Stapleton came from an extensive study prepared for Denver's Department of Parks and Improvements in 1948 by the bureaus of business and social research at the University of Denver and the University of Colorado. This report centered on civil aviation in the Denver area, and it also discussed the future of all aviation in Colorado. The study recommended long-range plans for the area development of aviation:

> It is apparaent that a growing metropolitan community which is a regional business center, a strategically located line on inter-regional air routes and an air transportation center of increasing importance, should study its existing aviation facilities, analyze its future needs and prepare a plan for the orderly development of adequate aviation facilities to secure maximum benefits from this newest form of transportation.

The study reported that Stapleton's terminal facilities were already inadequate, and that with a projected twentyfold increase in activity during the next 10 years, the airport would have difficulty surviving if it did not take action. Recommendations included the phasing out of private planes from Stapleton, expansion of all facilities (both terminal and runway) and the building of 20 new area airfields by 1970 to handle private aircraft.

Although the proposal and study were never acted on, one event in 1948 showed the seriousness of the congestion problem. City Councilman Ernest P. Marranzino, in June, called for the closing of Combs Air Park, located in the Park Hill area. Marranzino stated that the small planes landing and taking off at Combs were a danger to both residents and planes going in and out of Stapleton. He cited the fact that six small planes from Combs had crashed in the last year.

The movement to close down Combs grew until Harry B. Combs wrote to Mayor Newton informing him that on January 14, 1949, Combs Air Park would close down. Originally called Lowry Air Field, Combs Air Park was the oldest continually operated airport in Colorado. The Mountain States Aviation Company, which operated out of Combs, moved to Stapleton along with the other private plane owners who had used the old airport.

By early 1949, the south wing of the terminal was begun. On the May 9th edition of Mayor Newton's weekly radio show (station KLZ), he talked to Denver citizens about the construction. He explained again why he had to cancel the north wing and said the day was rapidly approaching when the airport would have to be totally self-supporting. His four-point plan called for: making the airlines and other users of the airport pay for their share of the cost of construction and maintenance; renting all possible space for airplane storage and parking; awarding airport concessions to the highest bidders; and developing sound business procedures for cost accounting, personnel policies and budgeting.

During his show, Newton pointed to the recent taxi concession as a good start in that direction. The city had sold a taxi franchise to the Airport Transport Company to exclusively cover the airport. The company would charge one dollar per person to the downtown area, and the city would get 10 percent of the gross revenues. The taxi company had 10 cabs and 8, 12-passenger limousines.

As 1949 drew to a close, Stapleton Airfield had 75 scheduled commercial flights a day and more than 400 nonscheduled private flights. The airport was number 16 in the United States for scheduled airline operations, and number 8 in total operations (commercial and general aircraft movements), with more than 25,000 takeoffs and landings a year.

*The need for more terminal space was evident in 1950, when 1,800-2,000 people passed through the airport every day and peak periods registered as many as 10,000 people per day. Courtesy of the* Denver Post.

# Chapter Four

By the early 1950s, the American people had totally accepted the airplane as a viable means of transportation, pushing to capacity commercial air carriers and airport facilities with their increasing use of the airplane. But the speed and ease of traveling long distances through the air was something not yet fully comprehended. There was still an element of magic in flying. The *Rocky Mountain News* captured this feeling in an article on January, 1950:

> They watch the shimmering airships roar on and off the light-lined runways. Their eyes watch, but their minds are still bewildered.
>
> But the miracle of the airplane best is summed up by the weary, out-of-patience mother near the glass window who intercepts her young son reaching with a grimy paw for a chocolate bar.
>
> "I told you no in New York, I told you no in Chicago, I'm telling you no in Denver, and when we get to Los Angeles, it will still be no."

With public acceptance of air travel in the 1950s, Stapleton experienced an unthinkable one million passengers in a single year (1955), more private plane congestion, multimillion dollar bond issues for further expansion and more negative reactions from local residents. But the single most important development to affect Stapleton in the 1950s was the coming jet age. Although jets would not begin flying regularly into Stapleton until 1959, the plans and proposed preparations for the new jetliners dominated the history of Stapleton during the mid- to late 1950s.

## Mayor Newton's Master Plan Goes Through Changes

At the beginning of the 1950s, Mayor Newton's master plan was once again in the news. Although the plan had been "finalized" in 1948, it was changed in 1949 (when the proposed north wing of the terminal was cancelled), and again in 1950. Figures for 1950 showed 1,800–2,000 people were passing through the terminal every day, with peak days registering nearly 10,000. This kind of passenger activity—with its corresponding increase in airplane activity—meant the airport needed more expansion than Newton had thought in 1948.

The problem, once again, was how to finance any necessary additions to the master plan? The 1948 plan had been financed through a $1.75 million bond issue Denver voters had approved that year, but this could not pay for the additions being contemplated in 1950. The CAA came to the rescue in April 1950, announcing it would match the bond issue money with its own funds, giving Denver a total of $3.5 million for expansion.

With this extra money, it was decided a new control tower could be built and the north wing put back in the master plan—although a finalized master plan would not be ready for city council approval until 1951.

During 1950, while the master plan was being refined, the south wing of the terminal—which had been started in early 1949—was completed. The structure's main feature was a restaurant and lounge on the second floor. The Sky Chefs Company had signed a lease on August 16, 1950, and moved in in October. The restaurant and lounge seated 386 and 52 people, respectively, with the dining room open from 11:30 A.M. to 10:00 P.M. and the lounge from 11:30 A.M. to 2:00 A.M. Despite temperance opposition, the company's application for a liquor license had been approved.

Sky Chefs, a subsidiary of American Airlines, already had 24 airport restaurants in operation by 1950. At Stapleton the company, employing 170 people, also operated a coffee shop (open all hours), a small bar on the first floor of the terminal, and catered for Western, Frontier and Braniff airlines. When all their facilities became operational, Sky Chefs served 2,000–2,500 people per day. In terms of airport revenues, the facilities contributed a substantial amount: In 1950 Stapleton's concessions generated $52,609; by 1951, with Sky Chefs operational, the concession revenues had jumped to $169,600.

Another project begun before Mayor Newton finalized the master plan, was the United Airlines office building, first proposed to the city council by United in 1948. The facility was to be constructed and attached to the northwest corner of the northern terminal wing. Denver bonds would pay for construction and the pay

The need for more terminal space was evident in 1950, when 1,800-2,000 people passed through the airport every day and peak periods registered as many as 10,000 people per day. Courtesy of the Denver Post.

By 1950 a south wing was added to the terminal. Courtesy of the Western History Department, Denver Public Library.

*The major feature of the new wing was a restaurant on the second floor operated by the Sky Chefs company. Windows covering the east wall afforded patrons a great view of airport operations. Courtesy of the Colorado Historical Society.*

*The need for more terminal space was evident in 1950, when 1,800-2,000 people passed through the airport every day and peak periods registered as many as 10,000 people per day. Courtesy of the* Denver Post.

*United and Continental airlines had become such important revenue sources for Stapleton by the 1950s that Denver, through bond financing, built them both hangars. Courtesy of the Western History Department, Denver Public Library.*

*On July 16, 1953, the new United office building was officially dedicated. The building was attached to the northwest corner of the terminal. Courtesy of the Western History Department, Denver Public Library.*

back would come from a 30-year lease at $89,780 a year. The building would be 67,000 square feet.

But before United's new office could actually be built, problems arose. When the CAA heard about the city's plan to build the structure, the agency cut Stapleton's $1.75 million appropriation to $800,000, stating it refused to pay for one-airline projects such as the United building.

This drastic action caused an immediate response from Denver. Mayor Newton promtly went to Washington to try and reverse the CAA's decision, successfully getting most of the money back. The *Rocky Mountain News* explained on December 22, 1950, "He [Newton] said the CAA was swayed from its earlier decision by the argument that Denver is not a city, state or regional airport, but a national one."

With the problem resolved, the United building was started. It was dedicated on July 16, 1953, and United moved its offices from hangar number five but retained its offices in hangar number three.

Mayor Newton's finalized expansion plan was submitted to the city council for approval on June 13, 1951. This plan called for a north wing made up of ticket counters and baggage, office and lobby space. There would also be a post office and cargo building, a canopy over the runway aprons in front of the terminal, a new control tower built on the canopy, passenger walkways to the loading areas, an observation deck and the remodeling of the old administration building to fit in with the south and north wings. Newton's plan was estimated to cost $3,342,154 (it ultimately cost $5 million), of which $280,000 would come from Denver's general fund, $1.75 million from the bond issue approved in 1948, $1,280,406 from the CAA and $70,000 from United Airlines as advance payment for its office building.

Both the original 1948 plan and the revised 1951 plan had called for remodeling the administration building to fit in with its two wings. But in early 1954, it was announced that with the completion of both wings, the administration building would be torn down and replaced as the final part of terminal expansion and improvement. This was necessary, it was felt, because the structure (the original building of the 1929 airport) was not fireproof and did not architecturally fit in with the two new wings. The new center section would be of red sandstone and have a 40-foot clock tower with a flyer's beacon on top. The first floor would be for lobby and concession space, the second floor for administrative and airline offices. Covered walkways would lead from the first and second floors to the open observation deck and passenger loading ramps.

While this master plan was being implemented, a plan to once again extend the east-west runway hit some snags. The extension meant closing down part of Havana Avenue and the people of Aurora did not like Denver's proposal to build a new road and have Aurora pay half the cost. Aurora said no and demanded Denver build two underpasses for the present road. Denver, realizing the cost of such underpasses, rejected the idea. A final solution came when Denver went to district court and had the land in question condemned. Aurora could do nothing more and Denver went ahead and extended the runway from 8,500 feet to 10,000 feet, completing the job in early 1953. High intensity landing lights, visible for 100 miles, were placed on the extended runway and the medium intensity lights previously used were moved to one of the diagonal runways, which had been using only flood lights. Stapleton was the first airport in the country to install such high intensity lights.

In February 1951, while the argument over the east-west runway was going on and the master plan was being revised, the taxi company, Airport Transit, cancelled its contract with the city. The company believed it was not making enough off the contract and wanted to resubmit a more lucrative bid. Unfortunately for Transit, the Yellow Cab Company also submitted a bid, which Denver accepted. Yellow Cab paid the airport seven percent of all its revenues, which came to approximately $865 a month, or $10,000 a year.

By 1956, however, the Dublix Cab Company challenged the city's right to sell an exclusive franchise at the airport. In early 1957, the Colorado Supreme Court ruled that the city was, indeed, in the wrong, and from then on any cab company could operate at the airport.

## Safety Measures Taken in the Early 1950s

In the early 1950s, Stapleton was not only growing through construction, it was growing in air activity. By 1951 there were 228,000 takeoffs and landings, compared to 64,300 in 1944, and more than 300,000 people either boarded or deplaned at Stapleton. During the next few years both passenger and airplane figures would increase by double-digit percentages.

This kind of activity called for constantly improving safety measures. In 1952, the CAA erected a new radar tower a few hundred yards northwest of Stapleton to better track aircraft activity. The new radar system had a backup power plant that could be automatically turned on if the city's power went out, and a rotating radar disc atop the tower was connected by underground cable to Stapleton's control tower.

The tower construction was lamented by the Denver media because the land being used was part of Lover's Knoll, a local teenage parking spot. An article in the July 23, 1952 *Rocky Mountain News* headlined, "Science has invaded another field—Lover's Knoll." It went on to report: "Lovers, young and old, will have to park their autos elsewhere from now on. There'll be no more hand holding or wrestling matches at Lover's Knoll."

A year after Lover's Knoll was leveled for the radar tower, Stapleton's new control tower became functional. Replacing the control tower atop the administration building, the new, $250,000 six-story tower was completed in June 1953. Built on the canopy in front of the terminal building, the tower had the latest in radar and radio receiving and transmitting equipment and would eventually house a radar room below the top of the tower which could track aircraft from 30 miles out. The CAA was in charge of all personnel in the tower and responsible for controlling the 750–800 planes—commercial, military and private—flying in and out of Stapleton every day.

The new control tower held great interest for many Denver citizens and on December 6, 1953, the *Denver Post* in the *Empire* section, ran an extensive article on it. The piece humorously termed the structure "the Tower of Babel" for the seeming confusion that reigned there: "Five minutes spent in the control tower convinces you that to be top-notch, an operator must have three heads, a radarscope in the seat of his pants, and the concentrative power of a bull caught in a cactus patch. . . . The rules prohibit him [the operator] from going crazy."

The peak period of activity, the article explained was from 2:00 P.M. to 8:00 P.M. To do their jobs properly, controllers had to be in constant contact with the Lowry tower, the federal traffic control center (still housed at Stapleton, but later moved to Longmont) and the communications center of every major airline operating out of Stapleton. Stapleton controllers also had the traffic gun—introduced in 1938—to control those planes without radios. The article concluded by stating that Stapleton Airfield, in its 24-year history, had not had a fatal airplane accident, an impressive fact for one of the top 20 airports in the country.

*Radar, developed during World War II, was utilized in controlling air traffic after the war and came to Stapleton Airfield in the early 1950s. Courtesy of the Colorado Historical Society.*

*In early 1953 the new six-story control tower was complete, taking the place of the tower atop the terminal building. The new tower was under the responsibility of the CAA, as were the 750-800 planes flying in and out of Denver a day. Courtesy of the* Denver Post.

*By 1954 expansion had brought about a north wing to the terminal. In this picture the old terminal can be seen between the south and north wing. Within a year the old terminal was razed and a new center section had been built. Courtesy of the* Denver Post.

## Mayor Newton's $5 Million Master Plan Completed

With the completion of the terminal center section in January 1955, the four-year, $5 million expansion program was finished. For the first time, people could claim their baggage from four carousels inside the terminal and could walk along covered passageways to their gates. An open observation deck gave a clear view of aircraft taking off and landing (142,655 people paid 10 cents each to go on it during the deck's first 18 months). More concessions and more lobby and ticket counter space reflected the better than fivefold increase in terminal size (the old terminal had been 7,500 square feet, the new one was 39,300 square feet). The *Denver Post*, on January 6, 1955, reported with pride: "The expansion, under Mayor Newton's direction, has converted the Denver air terminal into one of the best-appointed and most modern in the nation. It is so designed that it may be easily enlarged to meet future demands for additional space."

The official celebration marking the completion of the master plan took place on Sunday, June 19, 1955, with an open house from 9:00 A.M. to 6:00 P.M. All facilities were opened to the estimated 80,000–100,000 people who attended. Helicopter and plane rides over the city were offered, and by the end of the day 100 persons had gone aloft in a helicopter and 660 in an airplane. There were aviation exhibits and aircraft on review, including a six-engined B-47 and a 1912 open-cockpit plane. During the day's events, a helicopter rose to a national altitude record of 15,200 feet before being forced down by snow. The old record had been 13,800 feet. Newton, who would shortly be out of office, stated in the *Denver Post*, June 19, 1955: "Development of Stapleton is of vital importance to the growth of Denver and the public must remember that self-liquidating bonds for airport expansion are not a burden on the taxpayer. Stapleton now operates on a profit and is returning $200,000 a year back into the city's general fund."

Mayor Newton, it seems, was forewarning Denver citizens of the need for further expansion, even though his master plan had just been completed. The need for future master plans was evident, for by the end of 1955, Stapleton was growing in every conceivable way, from construction and acreage to number of passengers and air operations. The airport, by 1955, covered 1,850 acres and employed 3,100 workers (compared to 504 employees in 1946 and 2,500 in 1954) giving it the third largest payroll—excluding the state—in Colorado. More than 1,150,000 people passed through Stapleton in 1955 (a 19-percent increase over the year before), and more than 250,000 aircraft took off and landed,

making the facility the fifth busiest airport in the country.

A month before the June celebration, James C. Buckley, a terminal and transportation consultant from New York City, had turned in his report on the airport. Buckley had been commissioned by Denver a year and a half before to study the growth of Stapleton and recommend how the airport could handle its growth. Buckley's report stated that the passenger traffic by 1980 would reach an estimated 2,046,387 (in actuality, the 1980 figure was almost 10 times that number). This increase, Buckley believed, called for an immediate expansion program and long-range planning through 1980. There were two parts to Buckley's proposed plan: runway development and terminal/hangar development. He suggested both east-west and north-south runways be extended by 2,000 feet, which would require—in the case of the north-south runway—overpasses across Smith Road and the Union Pacific Railroad tracks. Buckley also suggested establishing a helicopter landing area, doubling the airline companies' wing of the terminal, building 200–400 room hotel facilities adjacent to the terminal, tripling the size of the terminal and purchasing as much land surrounding the airport as possible for future expansion. Taking these measures, Buckley concluded, would cost the city approximately $4.5 million through 1960.

## Private Planes—Benefit With Problems

Buckley's report stressed that the aircraft congestion being experienced at Stapleton would only increase during the coming years. Although nothing was specifically recommended in this report, later reports from Buckley would deal with the congestion problem. A great portion of this congestion came from private/business planes of the general aviation sector.

Nationally, statistics showed general aviation held a lead over commercial aviation in many ways: The 9,500 corporate planes in use by 1953 could seat 40,000 while total commercial aircraft could only seat 35,000. By 1954, general aviation flying time was one million hours more than all the flying time done by domestic commercial aviation.

This boom in general aviation—going on since 1946—had forced many major airports to ban small aircraft from their fields to relieve congestion. The smaller craft, while landing amid the larger commercial planes, caused traffic control problems because of their slower speeds. General aviation, when banned from larger airports, simply moved to smaller fields in the area that catered to it.

During the 1950s at Stapleton, general aviation accounted for one half of the total flight operations. In 1952, for example, local flights of private craft amounted

*On Sunday June 19, 1955 an open house was held for the completed $5 million expansion program that had taken four years to complete. More than 80,000 people attended. Courtesy of the* Denver Post.

*The expansion had included the north wing, which contained four baggage carousels, covered passage ways to the gates, an observation deck and additional ticket counters for the airlines. Courtesy of the Colorado Historical Society.*

During the four years of expansion, a decision had been reached to replace the old terminal with a new section that would have a clock tower. This section, complete with clock tower, can still be seen at the airport. Courtesy of the Colorado Historical Society.

William Nicholson, mayor from 1955-1959, was instrumental in increasing the airlines' landing fees, which in turn helped finance Stapleton Airport's move into the jet age. Courtesy of the Western History Department, Denver Public Library.

In October 1956 President Eisenhower came to Denver and many Denverites came to see him. Courtesy of the Denver Post.

Many of the private planes seen here had been flown from Oklahoma to Denver for the Oklahoma University/Colorado University football game on November 2, 1958. This reflected the growing number of private planes in use, which congested airways and airports around the country. At Stapleton in the late 1950s, general aviation was the fastest growing segment of the airport. Courtesy of the Denver Post.

to 123,991 operations (58.24 percent of the total), commercial air carriers had 52,221 (24.3 percent) and transient stopovers numbered 36,677 (17.23 percent). Because of these statistics, Stapleton was always sure of being in the top 10 or 20 airports in the country in flight operations.

Stapleton Airfield was, therefore, caught in a dilemma: ban small plane operation at the field to relieve congestion and lose both national standing and general aviation revenues or, let general aviation stay and have to continually build new facilities to house the planes and more runways to handle the congestion. Stapleton let general aviation stay.

During the early 1950s, private plane owners storing their planes at Stapleton began complaining about the treatment they and their planes were receiving. They called the small plane hangar facilities inadequate, citing the fact that many expensive business planes had to be kept out-of-doors because there was no available hangar space. In September 1952, Edgar G. Callahan, spokesman for the group and owner of a construction company, proposed to Mayor Newton and airport manager Dave Davis, that his company build small plane hangars at Stapleton. He would give them to the city in 10 years, and all he wanted was for Denver to give him the land to build them on, which would also be returned in 10 years. Callahan suggested the northwest corner of Stapleton as the perfect site for the general aviation hangars.

The mayor responded by stating he wanted all buildings at Stapleton to be city owned and, therefore, Callahan's 10-year ownership of the hangars was unacceptable. Newton did say, however, that something would be done for private plane owners, but only after completion of the major construction projects that were part of the master plan.

By early 1953, Denver's newspapers were running articles on the importance of the private plane industry to the city. A *Denver Post* article, May 31, 1953, stated, "America is doing business by air and the airplane—not only the commercial carrier but the smaller craft—puts Denver in closer contact with the people with whom it does business."

Also in 1953, there were two fixed-base operators at Stapleton who catered to private aircraft: Clinton Aviation and Combs Aviation. There were an estimated 100 private planes at Stapleton and half of them had no storage or hangar space. The Clinton and Combs hangars were simply too small for all the planes.

By 1955, private and business plane activity at Stapleton had increased 30 percent from the year before. There were now 200 general aviation aircraft at the airport, 92 of which were business planes—up from 69 business planes the year before. General aviation had become the fastest growing segment of aviation at the airport.

Finally, after years of waiting, private plane owners received some good news in August 1956. The city had decided to give 315,000 square feet of space, northwest of the terminal, for the building of 50 private plane hangars. Upkeep of the hangars would be the responsibility of the building firms, not the city, and the firms would lease the space for 20 years. The area provided for these hangars was just west of where Denver was building a hangar to be leased to one of the fixed-base operators for small aircraft sales and service. Completed in 1957, the city hangar was leased to Combs Aviation.

Upon hearing of Denver's plans for the hangars, private plane owners proclaimed the decision a boon to the development of general aviation at Stapleton. Through the rest of the 1950s, these aviation hangars satisfied most of the general aviation business. It would not be until the 1960s that the private plane sector and Denver would be embroiled in more arguments.

## Air Crashes Take Their Toll, Have Their Effect

The public popularity of flight during the 1950s called for increasing numbers of planes to be put into service, which in turn led to an increasing number of air crashes. These aviation accidents, while causing personal tragedy and industry loss, did have one positive effect. Citizen outcry over these crashes helped bring about stronger governmental controls and improved equipment, which ensured a higher standard of air safety.

In the early 1950s, the Denver metropolitan area was not untouched by aerial accidents: In the spring of 1950, an airplane crashed into a home in Aurora, killing the pilot and setting the house on fire; on December 3, 1951, a four-engine B-29 bomber dove into the "fashionable" Hilltop district east of Denver, killing eight crewmen, injuring seven others and burning five homes; the next day a United DC-3 cargo plane plowed into a field northeast of Denver near Rocky Mountain Arsenal, killing all three crew members; and on December 23, 1951, an Air Force B-25 bomber crashed on takeoff into an open field at East Bayaud Avenue and South Monaco Parkway, no one was killed.

Residents around the airport, particularly those in the heavily populated areas to the south and west, became more and more fearful of the situation as an increasing number of planes crashed. With Stapleton's runways, any plane taking off south on the north-south runway or west on the east-west runway would fly over residential areas. After every major crash, residents would once again voice their opinions that nothing was really being done to ensure their safety, and that everyone east of Denver was a potential target.

*As the airport grew during the 1950s, so did the threat of aviation accidents. Five of the firemen stationed at Stapleton stand before their trucks. From left to right: Ed Wester Kemp, Roland Matson, Lt. Mike Vecchio, Bob Barnard and Frank Glivar. Courtesy of the* Denver Post.

*To aid in safety in the skies, the CAA financed a new radar tower in the late 1950s that could track planes up to 50 miles away. Stapleton was only the fifth airport in the country to receive the radar tower. Courtesy of the* Denver Post.

Airport and CAA officials were trying their best to improve conditions at Stapleton through upgrading equipment and keeping the takeoffs and landings over residential areas to a minimum. In the late 1940s a ban had been established on airplanes taking off heading south, except when the wind was blowing 16 miles per hour or more from the south. This stipulation was made because with such a wind blowing, takeoffs eastward on the east-west runways would be too hazardous.

As for equipment, the CAA was implementing the most modern devices available in every major airport, including Stapleton, to cut the risks of flying and improve overall safety. At Stapleton, in January 1955, the CAA financed a new radar antenna to be placed atop a 70-foot tower, which would allow controllers to track all planes within a 50-mile radius and give them the ability to "stack" planes. As T. J. Holmes, the tower chief, explained to the *Rocky Mountain News:* "We have had to keep planes 100 miles apart while awaiting to land. Now, we can bring them in as close as 30 miles apart by watching them on the radar screen." The radar antenna and tower, located on the west side of Syracuse Street, would be operational by March. Stapleton was only the fifth city in the United States to receive the antenna.

Another measure taken by the CAA in 1955 was the reorganizing of Stapleton's air lanes to make the airport more efficient and to cut to a minimum the amount of flying over residential areas. The air lanes around Stapleton were like one-way streets on the ground, which meant that in many cases one plane could be waiting in the air or on the ground while another plane was taking off or landing in the same air lane. The CAA reorganized the system so that a plane could be landing in one air lane while another was taking off in another. This cut down the number of planes circling the airport waiting to land.

While Stapleton officials were coordinating efforts with the CAA to make the airport safer, the worst air crash of the 1950s occurred. One June 30, 1956, a United Airlines DC-7 and a TWA Constellation collided over the Grand Canyon, killing all 128 people aboard. Governmental efforts were redoubled in a drive for better national air safety.

In early 1958, the CAA announced that a new long-range radar system, the first in the country, would be installed 23 miles southeast of Denver. The 25-foot tower and 40-foot antenna would be in operation by July and have the ability to track planes in a 250-mile radius. The information from the system would be beamed by microwave to Stapleton.

Also, by the end of 1958, the CAA had placed new flashlight "strobeacons" of blue and white on the airport's north-south runway. Starting 3,000 feet from the end of the runway, the lights were placed every 100 feet to ensure visibility during bad weather. Stapleton was one of 19 airports around the country to receive the lights.

But even with the CAA's effort, the federal government decided to take more drastic measures to ensure air safety. In 1958, the government decided to form the Federal Aviation Agency (FAA) to replace the CAA (the CAB remained active) and the Airways Modernization Board. It was felt that the newly formed FAA would better serve air safety. The FAA was empowered through an act of Congress to enforce air safety and coordinate civilian and military use of airspace and establish air traffic controls and aids. The FAA was officially activated January 1, 1959.

The government and its aviation agencies knew how to respond to air crashes by upgrading airport and aviation standards and equipment, but in 1955 they faced a problem never experienced before: the sabotaging of an airplane. Denver has the dubious distinction of being the first U.S. city to experience such a situation. On the night of November 1, 1955, John Gilbert Graham, a student at the University of Denver, saw his mother off on United Airlines flight 629, bound for Seattle and carrying 44 people. Previously, Graham had placed a dynamite bomb in his mother's suitcase, and after her plane took off, he took out $37,500 worth of flight insurance—then waited.

More than 200 people saw the "ball of fire" in the sky near Longmont that a moment before had been Mrs. Graham's flight. The nose and tail of the DC-6B aircraft were found a mile apart. Local, state and federal investigators painstakingly pieced the craft back together, discovering a two-foot section next to Mrs. Graham's seat had disintegrated. Finding the flight insurance Graham had taken out on his mother, they took him into custody. After more than a year of trials, John Gilbert Graham went to his death on January 12, 1957. The *Denver Post* stated:

> With no display of emotion, he sat down in the death seat, sniffed at the hydrocyanic fumes, gasped for air, gave a scream and then lapsed into silence—forever. It took eleven minutes—the flying time from Denver to the Weld County scene of the crash of a plane he had sabotaged—before Graham was pronounced dead by prison doctors at 8:08 p.m.

The *Denver Post* also reported, on March 23, 1957, that there had been two bomb threats a few days before: one on a Continental flight and the other on a Western flight. The Western bomb threat caller had said, "There's enough dynamite on Flight No. 101 Western Airlines to blow up the entire country." Both were hoaxes, but nonetheless both planes were stopped and completely searched before being allowed to fly again.

Although these three incidents were merely previews of what was to come in the late 1960s and 1970s, when the airplane became a political tool of saboteurs and hijackers, they were seen by most people in the 1950s as isolated cases with no real future significance. It would only be in the late 1960s and 1970s that tight security measures became a part of every day air travel.

As for air crashes, during Stapleton's 30 years of operation, there had been no major air crash at the field. It would not be until a hot summer day in July 1961 that Stapleton would have to face that kind of tragedy.

## Stapleton Prepares for the Jet Age

Although the official jet age for Stapleton Airfield would not begin until May 1959, jets had begun appearing as commercial scheduled flights at major U.S. airports by 1958. Stapleton, city and airline officials knew that the airfield had to prepare and plan for this new advancement in aviation or face being left behind in national aviation standing.

The new jets created many problems. Because of their size and weight, they needed longer and stronger runways than conventional propeller planes. Also, because the jets were built to carry more people, Stapleton's terminal facilities would be inadequate for the anticipated increase in passenger traffic. Already, by the late 1950s, the terminal was overburdened by passengers being flown by the propeller planes. Everyone concerned agreed that something had to be done.

Groups were formed to study the problem and plans bantered around in the mid- to late 1950s on developing a comprehensive plan for Stapleton. In February 1956, a committee, composed of executives

*By the end of the 1950s the airport had one north-south runway, two parallel east-west runways, and two diagonal runways. Unfortunately, they were all inadequate for the regular use by jets, which were heavier than prop planes and needed more runway to takeoff on. The first jet came to Stapleton on March 12, 1957 by accident, landing because of a snow storm, but the first regularly scheduled jet took off from Stapleton on May 6, 1959. It took off intentionally underloaded because Stapleton's runways were all too short. Courtesy of the Colorado Aviation Historical Society.*

from the six major commercial air carriers, was formed to discuss how to expand and improve Stapleton to meet jet age requirements. Two months later, the CAA called for studies to be done by the airport on how the coming jet age would affect it. On November 21, 1956, the *Rocky Mountain News* reported two more studies in the works. One was being done by Stapleton consultant Buckley and the other by United Airlines. They would both be completed within a few weeks. Mayor Nicholson remarked to the paper: "I honestly don't know if Stapleton can handle jet-airliners. There are many conflicting reports and continual experiments with jet airliners."

Many people thought that the Buckley and United reports would suggest moving the airport because of the estimated cost of modernizing Stapleton—some estimates ran as high as $35 million—and because the airport lacked the necessary expansion land. When both reports were submitted to the mayor in January 1957, they agreed Stapleton could stay where it was but with certain necessary changes. Both reports called for extensions of runways, but Buckley's recommended the main east-west while United felt the north-south should be extended. The reports did agree that Stapleton needed a new north-south runway, and that runway improvements and construction could run as high as $18-$22 million. After reviewing both reports, Mayor Nicholson told the *Rocky Mountain News* on January 11, 1957: "I am extremely relieved that both reports advise against relocating the field. But I am certain Denver taxpayers will not approve general obligation bonds to pay for the necessary improvements. The people in the airline industry will have to foot the bill for the improvements."

For the airlines, footing the bill meant increased office rents and landing fees. The airport had been charging the same landing fees for the scheduled air carriers since the 1940s, based on the number and type of aircraft flown in and out of Stapleton. Both Continental and United had contracts, negotiated in the 1940s and good through 1966, that had payment equivalent to three cents per 1,000-airplane pounds landing at Stapleton. The 1,000 pounds did not include passenger or cargo weight, just the airplane's manufactured weight. The four other commercial airlines at Stapleton (Braniff, Western, Frontier and TWA) had no contracts but were paying the same rates.

According to a Buckley financial report in 1956, Stapleton received, in 1955, only $56,768 in landing fees when it should have received $580,300. Buckley recommended fees be increased to 22.5 cents per 1,000 pounds—a whopping 700 percent increase—citing New York City's airport fee of 35 cents per 1,000 pounds.

After reviewing Buckley's fee recommendations, Mayor Nicholson announced the airport would increase the fees of Frontier, Braniff, Western and TWA, and

hoped United and Continental would voluntarily drop their contracts to help support the improvement plans. Mayor Nicholson also said that if landing fees were upped, it would mean—in all fairness to the airlines— that existing facilities would have to be improved and new ones built. Because of this statement and Denver's intention to prepare Stapleton for the jet age, Continental and United agreed, in December 1956, to voluntarily raise their landing fees, though they both felt 10 or 15 cents was more reasonable than Buckley's 22.5 cents. By the end of 1957, however, both airlines were backing away from their position because no real work had yet been started to improve Stapleton's facilities.

Stapleton's landing fees did not automatically change with Mayor Newton's announcement in 1956. The relationship between Denver's airport and the airlines was one of mutual dependency—without one the other could not survive. Because of this relationship, the mayor realized the airlines should have their say in what they felt would be fair landing fees. The meetings covering this topic continued through the late 1950s, and it was not until the 1960s that the airlines at Stapleton officially began paying higher rates—but only 9-13 cents per 1,000 pounds.

The landing fee topic created a great deal of friction between Denver officials and airline executives during the years of debate. Throughout the 1950s, as Stapleton was attempting to grow and change to meet the developing aviation industry, tension grew between all those involved with the airport. In 1954 Mayor Newton proposed, for the first time, a possible solution to the problems between the two groups. On April 14, Newton spoke to the *Denver Post* about his idea: "Mayor Newton said Saturday if Stapleton field continues to grow as it has in the past few years he favors creation of a Denver airport authority. The authority, similar to port authorities in coast cities, would supervise the airfield and city aviation operations on a non-political basis."

Under this plan, Stapleton's revenues would not be returned to the city's general fund, but placed in a separate fund for the exclusive use by the airport. Since its beginnings in 1929, Stapleton's revenues went into the general fund, from which Stapleton's allocations also came. This meant that revenues generated at Stapleton could be used for other city projects financed from the general fund. An airport authority was popular with the commercial and general aviation sector, for they felt their interests would be better served by an organization that had no political ties or affiliations.

In early 1957, Nicholson—who had kept Newton's idea alive—appointed a 10-member committee called the Airport Citizens Committee to study the possibility of creating such an airport authority. Through their recommendations, the city attorney began, in June 1958, to work on a charter amendment creating the authority. The proposed amendment would have to first be voted on by the city council, then presented to Denver voters for their approval.

Through the remainder of the 1950s, the idea was tossed around. An airport authority was never created as Mayor Newton originally envisioned, but in 1960, an ordinance was passed prohibiting use of airport funds for anything but the airport.

## The Rocky Mountain Arsenal Land Problem

With not even a jet age master plan finalized in 1957, Stapleton found itself accidently hosting its first jetliner on March 12. At 11:50 A.M. a prototype Boeing 707, carrying aviation writers and Boeing officials on a flight across country, made an emergency landing at Stapleton because of a snowstorm. It had flown from Chicago in only two hours and six minutes—a conventional propeller plane would have made the trip in four hours. Although the aircraft had been banned from LaGuardia airport because it was too noisy, no one at Stapleton seemed to notice when it touched down (though jet noise would be a continuing point of controversy between the airport and residents in years to come).

One jet, though, did not make a jet age; it would be two more years before Stapleton began serving regularly scheduled jets. But airline and airport officials knew time was running out if the airport was to be ready. While many were pushing for the development of a master plan, others saw the need for immediate action as well. In 1958, the CAA came to the rescue by giving Denver $34,469 for immediate repairs and improvements until a master plan was finalized. The airport's taxiways and field apron were widened to accommodate the jetliners' longer wingspans, and in August 1959, the main east-west runway was resealed with asphalt.

But these were only stopgap measures, a jet age master plan had to be developed. Although experts disagreed on many points of the proposed plan, they all agreed that stronger and longer runways were needed for the jets, more terminal space and facilities were needed for passsengers and a new north-south jet runway had to be built.

The airport, in the late 1950s, had one 7,400-foot north-south runway, two parallel east-west runways and two diagonal runways. Although some of these would have to be extended and strengthened to handle constant jet traffic, the biggest topic of discussion by 1957 was the building of a new north-south jet runway.

Because of the runway congestion in front of the terminal building, all experts agreed the only place to put a new north-south runway would be northeast of the existing north-south runway. In June 1958, two master plans, scheme A and scheme E, had been developed for

possible runway construction. Scheme A, an immediate plan for quick jet age preparation, involved building one 12,000-foot north-south runway extending into Rocky Mountain Arsenal land. Scheme E, a long-range plan covering the next 12–15 years, called for more drastic measures. It included three 12,000-foot runways on Arsenal land: two north-south and one east-west. A large terminal building would also be built on Arsenal land to handle the flow of planes and passengers, making Stapleton a kind of two airports in one. Both plans depended completely on receiving Arsenal land.

Considering Denver's history of obtaining Arsenal land, both plans seemed doomed from the start. But with no other source of available land for expansion, it was Stapleton's only hope. In 1954, the city had asked for 252 acres of Arsenal land when a new runway was initially discussed. A few years later, when the future impact of the new jet age on Stapleton was fully comprehended, however, Denver increased its request to 3,000 acres—1,800 immediately and the rest later. In 1958, Mayor Nicholson was even reported as saying that what Stapleton ultimately needed was all of the Arsenal *and* Buckley Airfield to implement scheme E.

While Denver's requests were going through the government bureaucracy, the Air Force, in 1957, also requested 2,000 acres of Arsenal land for a proposed nuclear propulsion laboratory and promised Denver the land necessary to build a north-south jet age runway if it was granted the 2,000 acres. By March of that year, the Air Force was told it would receive the 2,000 acres and immediately told Denver it would get 1,000 feet of land on each side of the center of the proposed north-south runway.

But this promise was followed by more than a year of infighting among the Air Force, the Army, the CAA and Denver before a settlement was reached. On November 20, 1958, the Army agreed to give the Air Force 1,770 acres, of which Denver would receive 180 acres. Mayor Nicholson went on record as still wanting the 3,000 acres requested earlier, but said he would not argue about it then, because he had years to discuss the additional acreage with everyone concerned.

As the details of the agreement were being worked out, however, another obstacle appeared: the newly formed FAA. In March of 1959, the FAA rejected, temporarily, any transfer of Arsenal land to Denver. The FAA felt Denver's scheme E was far too ambitious and, in a letter to Nicholson, stated that approval of the 180-acre parcel would imply FAA acceptance of Denver's long-range plan. The agency concluded by writing it would have to study the whole issue before agreeing to any part of the plan.

Because of this action, on April 5, 1959, it was announced that Denver would cut back its requests to only 657 acres—the 1954 request of 252 and a new request of 405—just enough for a north-south runway.

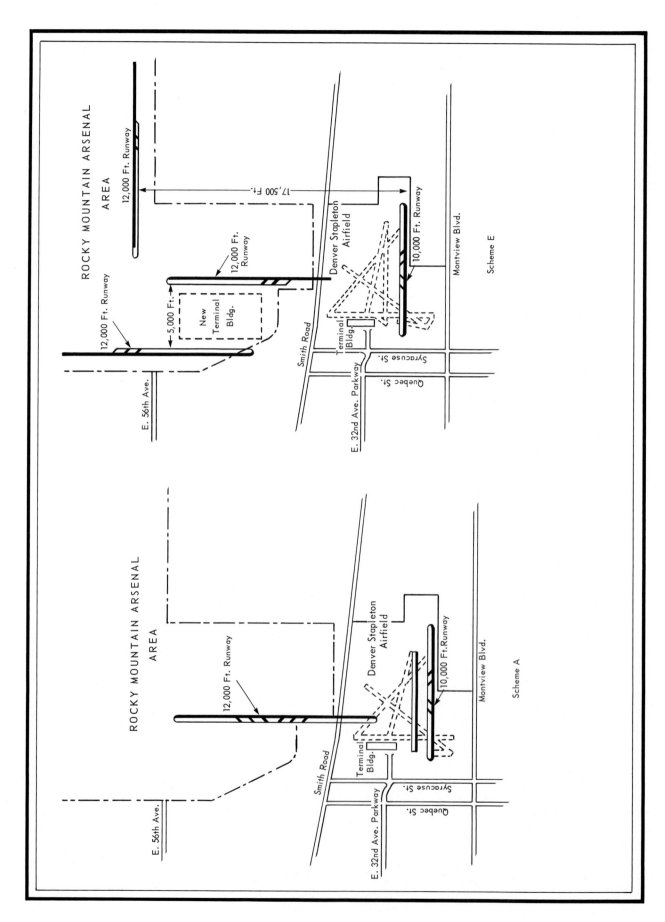

Two days later, on April 7, Denver finally received the deed to the original 1954 request of 252 acres. The land was north of Smith Road and the Union Pacific Railroad tracks, between Yosemite and Havana streets. The 405-acre parcel was north of that.

Viewing the acquisition of 252 acres as tacit approval for a new north-south runway, Denver voters approved a $20 million bond issue in May 1959 to finance the project. The airlines had been totally opposed to the bond issue for fear that their landing fees—still three cents per 1,000 pounds—would be drastically increased to pay for the retirement of the bonds.

Meanwhile, the FAA was conducting tests to determine if Stapleton would benefit more by building a new runway or by extending the existing ones. The agency brought a giant simulator and monitors to Stapleton which were designed to create flying conditions and flight patterns on different imaginary runways. The tests showed that building a new north-south runway would be the best course of action, giving air controllers at Stapleton the ability to handle 79 airplanes per hour as compared to the actual 30 planes per hour being handled during 1959 peak times.

To add to the confusion already surrounding Stapleton's growth plans, on April 10, 1959, Buckley submitted recommendations for a master plan. The report, which had taken 17 months to complete, called for land acquisition, a helicopter landing area, expansion of the terminal, freight and landing facilities and construction of a north-south runway starting northeast of the terminal building and crossing the Union Pacific tracks, Sand Creek and the proposed Highway 40 (which later became Interstate 70).

Dick Batterton, the new mayor who had been manager of public works under Mayor Nicholson, decided on Buckley's runway plan on August 12, 1959. Being somewhat strong-willed, Batterton announced that the city would go ahead with the runway even though the additional 405 acres necessary for the runway had not been turned over to the city.

In October, 1959, the Army agreed to release the land to Denver. Instead of the 405 acres requested, though,

the Army said it would turn over 623 acres—218 of which could not be used, but was given for airspace—to make the total acreage for a new runway 875 acres. Mayor Batterton said it was the happiest news he had received since he took office in July. He estimated that work would begin on the runway in April or May 1961. (As was typical with Arsenal land deals, however, Denver only received 427 acres of the promised 623 on February 26, 1960.)

## The Jet Age Comes to Denver

On May 6, 1959, the jet age came to Stapleton with the takeoff of the first regularly scheduled jetliner. The Continental Boeing 707, with 93 people aboard, also held the distinction of carrying the most people on a single flight in the history of the field. Stapleton's lack of proper jet age preparation, however, was reflected in the fact that the jet was purposefully underloaded because the airport's runways were too short for a fully loaded jet takeoff.

With the planned construction of a new north-south runway, though, that situation would be remedied by the early 1960s. But a runway was not the only part of Stapleton's planned growth. On November 20, 1959, a scale model of the proposed four-story terminal facilities was unveiled at City Hall. For the past year the terminal master plan was kept secret while details were being worked out, but at last Denver citizens discovered what was in store for the terminal. There would be a new main terminal section connected on the west with the present ticketing wing, a car ramp leading to the second floor of the terminal and a new control tower that planners hoped would not have to be built if the existing tower could be incorporated into the new plans.

Also represented in the model was the recently completed parking lot in front of the terminal. In 1958 the old lot plus 3,000 feet of East Twenty-second Avenue was torn up and a new parking lot of 650,000 square feet, with a capacity of 1,000 cars, was built. A covered walkway the length of the lot was also constructed. A new roadway to the airport was built, and the old meters in the lot were taken out. A Cleveland firm, Airport Parking, operated the new lot and gave the city, annually, 85.3 percent of gross revenues or $100,000, whichever was greater.

At the unveiling of the terminal model, airline executives were asked to review the sketches and suggest any improvements they deemed necessary before the final plans were drawn up.

As the decade of the Fifties came to a close, Stapleton was once again moving in a positive direction to meet the challenge thrown at it by the constantly evolving aviation industry.

*By June 1958 the coming jet age so worried city and airport officials that two plans were formulated to prepare Stapleton for the future. "Scheme A" proposed a 12,000-foot north-south runway extending into the Rocky Mountain Arsenal, while "Scheme E" was a long-range plan proposing two 12,000-foot north-south runways and one 12,000-foot east-west runway — all on Arsenal land. Courtesy of Stapleton International Airport.*

*One of the many planes that flew in and out of Stapleton during the early 1960s. Courtesy of the Colorado Historical Society.*

# Chapter Five

With the master plan of the 1950s under way in the early 1960s, Stapleton entered the new decade determined to upgrade its facilities. The necessity for such improvement was evident in the 1960 statistics: nationally, Stapleton ranked eighth in itinerate (stopover) plane operations; sixteenth in scheduled air carrier operations; fourth in general aviation movements; and fifth in total aircraft operations, with more than 1.5 million passengers boarding or deplaning at the airport. By 1961, Stapleton had jumped to third place in total operations and second in general aviation activity, while passengers exceeded 2 million.

This growth, and the potential for more, lent an air of desperation to the 1960s as city and airport officials attempted to improve facilities at a pace equal to the increasing number of passengers and aircraft. But as they worked toward this goal, officials faced continuing problems with master plan revisions, citizen protests, Arsenal land disputes and general aviation congestion.

## The Master Plan is Revised Again

An important consideration throughout these struggles was the commercial air carriers operating out of Stapleton. The city could not afford to alienate this important segment for it supplied much of the airport's revenues. These carriers were already somewhat disillusioned with the airport because of its slow response to the jet age in the 1950s. In an effort to appease these companies, the master plan of the late 1950s was once again revised, evolving into two phases. Phase one—already underway in 1960—included the new north-south runway; a new control tower, fire station, and cargo building; and site grading and drainage for the new general aviation area. This phase would be completed by 1962. Phase two of the master plan included the expansion of the terminal buildings and construction of two "fingers," or concourses—now known as concourse B and concourse C. These two, each 800 feet long, would increase the number of airline gates at Stapleton from 15 to 32. Phase two was planned for completion in mid-1966.

On February 26, 1960, while the master plan was being divided into the two phases, Denver received 427 acres of Arsenal land, the last tract of land necessary for the new north-south runway. Work was begun immediately on the runway's three overpasses crossing Sand Creek, Interstate 70 and the Union Pacific Railroad tracks.

The I-70 overpass—a two-lane tunnel/bridge 565 feet long and costing a quarter of a million dollars—was dedicated by Mayor Batterton on November, 1961. Because of the bridge and new runway, Smith Road was permanently closed to through traffic between Syracuse and Havana streets.

Construction of the other two overpasses was completed shortly after that and the runway was progressing on schedule in 1961/1962, until problems arose with two of the three bridges. Only nine months after the I-70 overpass had been dedicated, cracks began appearing in both the I-70 and Union Pacific overpasses. The cracks were so bad on the 750-foot Union Pacific tunnel that the company refused to run trains through it until repairs were made. Although experts agreed the bridges were structurally sound, blame for the cracks ranged from normal settling to poor design. The cost of repairing both bridges came to more than $10,000 and took three months to complete. The Sand Creek overpass had no such problems because it was of a different design.

During September 1962, the month the cracks were discovered, the *Rocky Mountain News* ran a story on the progress of the master plan's phase one. The airport had already spent more than the $20 million generated by the bond issue approved in the 1950s. An emergency $1 million had been tacked on to the original $20 million bond in the 1950s, but that, too, was already spent. In total, by September 1962, $23,155,589 had been used on the master plan. The overage was covered, the newspaper reported, only because the federal government had allocated more funds than the city had expected in the 1950s.

But this did not stop the *Rocky Mountain News* from criticizing how the airport had implemented the master plan and spent the money. The same day the paper ran the story, it also ran an editorial headlined, "Headache at the Airport." The piece stated:

In the 1960s international flights became reality. Here is the dedication of TWA's first flight from Europe to Denver in 1960. Officially, Denver did not become an international airport until December 1, 1968, when Western Airlines flew non-stop from Calgary, Alberta Canada to Stapleton. Courtesy of the Colorado Historical Society.

One of the many planes that flew in and out of Stapleton during the early 1960s. Courtesy of the Colorado Historical Society.

*The clock tower center section of the terminal, which had taken the place of the original terminal, had become a recognizable part of the airport by the early 1960s. Courtesy of the Colorado Aviation Historical Society.*

*Stapleton, in 1960, was ranked fifth in total aircraft operations, and more than 1.5 million people boarded or deplaned that year. The following year the airport jumped to third place in total plane operations and more than 2 million people pased through the airport. These figures were best represented by the fact that the terminal always seemed full of people. Courtesy of the Denver Post.*

The "master plan" that was being constantly changed and updated through the 1950s, went through more changes in the 1960s. In 1960 the concept of a four-story terminal to relieve congestion, and a 14-story control tower attached to a 217-room hotel, were proposed. The terminal and tower were built but the hotel never materialized. *Courtesy of the* Denver Post.

In 1962, only nine years after the six-story control tower had been built, the new 14-story control tower became operational. Also completed in 1962 was a new 20-bed fire station and a new north-south jet runway. By January 1964, as the picture shows, the new concourses, B and C, were being constructed as phase two of the master plan. *Courtesy of the* Denver Post.

Denver is suffering a gigantic headache in its plodding efforts to achieve a jet age airport.

For all our expensive consultants, designers, contractors, supervisors and political sponsors we can't seem to ward off continual attacks of fumbleitis and additional spending.

There is no time to be wasted while the finger pointing and the argument over responsibility goes on. The city has expert consultants—employed at high fees—to do this job.

Let's see they get their work done fully and completely—and now.

By the end of 1962, phase one of the master plan was complete: a new runway, fire station and control tower; site grading and drainage for the general aviation area; a cargo building; and the purchase of a new snowblasting machine that could clear the runways in 90 minutes.

The runway, costing $7 million, was more than 2 miles long (11,500 feet) and 150 feet wide, and with its 10-inch concrete base could handle the largest jets. The new fire station, which the FAA had helped pay for, was located on the south side of Smith Road near the new north-south runway and housed four trucks and a 20-bed dormitory. The control tower, costing $684,072, was 14 stories high (170 feet), as opposed to the old tower that had been six stories high (80 feet), and its elevators and stairs were designed so that in the future they might be used in conjunction with a hotel built around it.

The idea of a control tower/hotel had been thought of in 1960 as a way of helping finance the tower. The hotel would occupy seven stories of the structure (with a 217-room capacity), while the first three floors of the tower would go to Sky Chefs, and the top three floors would be used by the FAA for the actual control tower.

A hotel/control tower was part of the growing desire by the Denver City Council in the 1960s to attract ancillary services and companies to the airport and surrounding area. By 1963, the council had passed an ordinace to rezone the land around Stapleton for commercial use—Ramada Inn Corproation had expressed interest in erecting a hotel near the airport. At the time, there were only three hotels in a two-mile radius, while other major airports had many more. Mayor Tom Currigan, however, did not like the idea of rezoning and vetoed the measure, but was overriden by the council. An injunction placed on any construction was overruled by a Denver district court. Finally, in 1965, the Colorado Supreme Court reversed the lower court's decision, explaining that the original city ordinance had been illegal because the city council had failed to give proper public notice and hold enough hearings. In September 1965, a new—and properly handled—zoning ordinance was passed by the council. A Ramada Inn, as well as a Holiday Inn, began rising on the west side of Quebec, between East Thirty-fifth and East Thirty-eighth streets. This was the beginning of substantial commercial construction around the airport.

While arguments continued in the early 1960s over rezoning, the *Denver Post* ran an article on phase two of the master plan in August 1963. Construction of the two fingers, the paper reported, was right on schedule, but they were now going to be 1,200 feet long rather than the original 800 feet, to provide more airline gates. The article went on to report: "The terminal building expansion, expected to cost about $4 million, will double the present 100,000 square feet of space. The project will connect the new tower and loading fingers and extend east and north on a broad arc. It is scheduled for completion late in 1966."

By April 1964, however, phase two was being modified once again. Working with the commercial airlines, city officials had decided to temporarily shelve plans for moving walkways in both concourse B and C until the airlines could determine whether or not they were needed. They ultimately decided against them—moving walkways would not be seen at Stapleton until the 1970s, when concourse D was built.

Also under discussion in April 1964 was additional parking. Some city council members felt that the planned second-level, 800-car roofless parking lot was unnecessary, but airport officials convinced them of its worth. A month later, the council agreed to let Newsview Theaters, Inc., build a 175-seat theater between the new control tower and the restaurant. The movie theater was not built, however, until April 1966, and then it was only a 50-seat movie lounge called Skyport Cinema. The theater, located on the mezzanine level, was open seven days a week from 11:00 A.M. to 9:00 P.M. and showed travelogue-short subject films. It was closed in the early 1970s because the airport needed more and more space.

## Denver Once Again Goes After Arsenal Land

By early 1962, Mayor Batterton realized that if Stapleton was to keep pace with aviation's growth, it would need more land for further expansion. The problems over Arsenal land in the 1950s had not deterred Denver from hoping to get more land. Batterton requested 1,355 acres of Arsenal land declared surplus by the Army in October 1961 from the General Services Administration (GSA). This land was requested in two parcels, one 881.65 acres and the other 474 acres, both lying on either side of the new north-south runway that was then under construction. In a letter to the GSA, according to the *Denver Post* of January 23, 1962, Batterton wrote: "[the land] is vital to the continued growth and development of Stapleton Field. It is readily

*By August 1964 the new concourses were inching their way toward where the new four-story terminal would be built. Courtesy of the* Denver Post.

apparent that the only direction the airport can be expanded between 1970 and 1985 is to the north."

Batterton also pointed out to the GSA that plans were presently being formulated to build another north-south runway 8,000 feet east of the present one under construction, and the requested land would give Stapleton the needed safety and sound zones for the second north-south runway.

But, as usual, land acquisition did not go well for Denver. After years of arguments with various governmental agencies, the GSA put the land up for sale in 1964, and Denver had to buy it. But the city was only able to purchase 805 acres on the west wide of the north-south runway.

Although Denver had not received all the land it wanted, there was still hope that more land would come in the future. Plans were made for the second north-south runway. It was initially planned to cross I-70, as the other north-south had done, but with the extra cost of building another bridge and with the constant demands by local residents to place it further north, the

proposed runway was moved north of I-70, deep into Arsenal land. It would be parallel with the then completed north-south runway and be 13,500 feet long. Before it would be built in the 1970s, however, Denver would again have to come to grips with the Rocky Mountain Arsenal over land.

## Stapleton's First Major Air Crash

During the early 1960s, as Denver was attempting to get land from the Arsenal and implementing phase one of the master plan, tragedy struck. On July 11, 1961, at four minutes past noon, a United Airlines DC-8, flight 859 out of Philadelphia with 113 passengers and seven crew, crashed at Stapleton. On the approach to the airport's major east-west runway, a hydraulic problem was discovered. The pilot—making what many felt later to be a fatal mistake—did not call for emergency equipment to meet the plane. As the craft touched down, traveling at 120 miles per hour, it began a skid that blew out two tires. Veering off the runway, the plane crossed a stretch of field before its starboard wingtip hit a foot high, 30-inch concrete slab—part of a taxiway construction site on the other east-west runway. The fuel tank ripped open, igniting jet fuel and sending flames 100 feet into the sky, as the plane crashed into a truck parked on the runway. The truck's driver, who was eating his lunch, was killed instantly. The plane's passengers escaped through forward hatches until flames enveloped the entire craft. The blaze was so intense that within moments the portside of the plane had literally melted. In all, 17 people were killed and 84 injured. It was the worst air crash in Stapleton's history, and still holds that distinction.

The surrounding area reacted quickly and completely. Ten city trucks and more than 300 Denver policemen and firemen responded, Lowry sent personnel and equipment, and doctors went on alert at Colorado and Denver General hospitals. Airport and airline personnel from corporate executives to grounds keepers—many of whom had witnessed the crash—ran out to aid in rescue work. The two helicopters at Stapleton flew injured to hospitals, while police cleared the streets to and from the airport for ambulances and fire trucks. Smiley Junior High's gym was used as a temporary morgue. Throughout the day cooperation, heroism and sacrifice could be seen everywhere.

Blame, accusations and criticism, however, began to surface the following day. The fire department was hardest hit by criticism, not for how the firemen performed—there was only praise for these men—but for the lack of modern equipment. The *Rocky Mountain News* reported, "Denver firemen Tuesday faced a jet age crash with propeller age equipment."

At the time of the accident, Stapleton had only three trucks and seven men on duty. One truck was a water carrier, one a low pressure fog unit and one a high pressure fog unit—all inadequate for a jet fuel fire. A modern truck with foam was sent from East Thirty-eighth and Pontiac, and Lowry and Buckley fields sent their equipment, but all arrived too late to be effective.

Ironically, Denver had been arguing for more than a year over what fire equipment should be at the airport and bids had just been opened for new equipment the day before the crash. Also, phase one of the master plan called for construction of a new firehouse, but it would only be completed in 1962. Two days after the crash, it was revealed that safety manager, John M. Schooley, had written the city three times during the past two years warning that Stapleton's fire equipment was inadequate for a jet crash and fire.

After the crash, city efforts to modernize Stapleton's fire-fighting equipment were redoubled. On July 19, Mayor Batterton reported that until the city did buy new equipment, Stapleton would have the use of an Air Force foam truck that was being flown in from Big Spring, Texas. By the end of 1961, Denver had ordered two new trucks and in August 1962 the first arrived. The truck had a pumping capacity of 800 foam gallons per minute and 1,500 gallons of water per minute. The newspapers reported that the arrival of the truck had relieved tension that another crash might occur before Stapleton could modernize.

More than two years after the crash, the accident was again in the news. On November 11, 1963, FAA administrator, N. E. Halaby, on a radio program called "Washington Viewpoint" in Washington, D.C., mentioned the Stapleton crash as part of the reason why the FAA was initiating certain requirements for better air safety. These requirements included training flight crews on emergencies, slide chutes for passengers and, as Halaby was quoted as saying in the *Rocky Mountain News* November 12, "Firemen who don't just pitch horseshoes but know how to get into a cabin of an airplane and let people escape."

But this was not all the FAA was doing to aid in better air safety. The organization was constantly trying to improve technological features at airports around the country. Only five months after the United Airlines crash, the FAA installed new red and white glide slope indicator lights in 40 airports, including Stapleton. The lights were two sets of bars located on both sides of a runway, with the first set of bars 70 feet down the runway and the second 700 feet down the runway. If an aircraft's approach was correct, the first set would appear white and the second red. If the plane was too low, both would appear red, and, if too high, the pilot would see both bars as white. The lights, developed by the British Royal Aircraft Establishment, could be seen 5 miles away in daylight and 15 miles away at night.

In 1962, the FAA established one of the most important features to aid traffic flow and safety around Stapleton—the Longmont facility. An FAA center controlling traffic throughout the region had been at Stapleton since 1942, but with Stapleton's growth, the FAA decided to move the control center to Longmont. From the facility, the FAA would control all air traffic in a five-state region and determine when to pass control over to Stapleton controllers. The facility, dedicated in June 1962, was called the Denver Air Route Air Traffic Control Center, and it housed more than $3 million of electronic equipment to track planes.

To better aid the air controller at Stapleton, the FAA also installed new radar screens late in 1962. With the old screens, the controllers had to mark each aircraft blip with a grease pencil in order to chart the plane's flight pattern. The new screens stored these blips, then showed a continuous line, which was the plane's flight path. Also, a map of the area could be superimposed on the screens to give the controllers accurate readings of aircraft location.

Immediately following this development, the FAA

# Rocky Mountain News

A Scripps-Howard Newspaper

Colorado's First Newspaper—Founded in 1859

103D YEAR: NO. 81    Entered as second class matter, postoffice, Denver. Published every morning by Denver Publishing Co.   DENVER 1, COLO., WEDNESDAY, JULY 12, 1961

SUNRISE
EDITION
★★★★
FORECAST:
Partly Cloudy
PRICE 5 CENTS
88 PAGES

## 4 Pages of Crash Pictures in Center of Paper

# 17 DIE, 84 HURT IN CRASH OF JET

## Faulty Hydraulic System Is Blamed; Fire Equipment Inadequate

—STORIES AND PICTURES ON PAGES 5, 6, 8, 10, 11, 12, 14, 17, 19, 22, 28, 30, 34, 43, 44, 45, 46 AND 61

Smoke billows from United jetliner that crashed Tuesday in landing at Stapleton Airfield.

—Rocky Mountain News Photo by Mike O'Meara.

announced it would erect a new, more effective radar tower at Stapleton. It would be only 20 feet high, but it would replace the 70-foot radar tower west of Stapleton that had been in operation since 1955.

## Citizen Reaction to the Growing Airport

All of these measures, from new fire trucks to radar screens and towers, improved the efficiency and safety at Stapleton Airfield. But for many local residents, they were not enough. These residents had two major concerns: jet noise and air safety.

On October 18, 1960, the Park Hill Development Association called for a halt of all flights on the major east-west runway because of the noise and continual flying over the area. Airport officials again stated—as they had done in the 1950s—that they were doing their best to limit the number of planes using the east-west runway under the 1940s runway restriction plan, but shutting down the runway completely was simply impossible. They also told Park Hill residents that once the new north-south runway was complete, planes would be using it more often than the east-west, thus, alleviating much of the noise and safety problems.

Many local residents accepted these statements, believing the north-south runway would bring about a change for the better. The runway was completed in 1962, and Park Hill people waited for the change that was supposed to come. By January 1963, however, a *Denver Post* poll found Park Hill residents still mad about the noise and planes flying over their area. They had begun calling Twenty-sixth Avenue the "26th Avenue Express" because planes were still roaring over the street on their approach to Stapleton. Many residents told the *Denver Post* that there was no significant reduction of noise and that aircraft were flying as low as 300–400 feet over Park Hill.

Citizens began to take specific action. Eight East Denver residents, in two individual suits, took Denver to court for the value loss of their homes experienced since jets had appeared. The houses were all in a direct line with the east-west runway, and the eight felt that they had lost from $3,500 to $15,000 on their homes. Collectively, they sought $353,550 in damages, claiming the airport had said the problems were only temporary until the north-south runway was built. The two cases went to U.S. District Court at the same time and in

*On July 8, 1961, at four minutes past noon, Stapleton Airfield suffered its worst air disaster when a United Airlines DC-8 crashed on approach to the airport's major east-west runway. In all, 17 people died and 84 were injured. From this unfortunate accident, however, better safety measures did come to Stapleton. Excerpt from the* Rocky Mountain News.

February 1965, the court ruled in favor of the homeowners.

Two years later, on May 22, 1967, a meeting was held by Park Hill residents who wanted to unite under the Park Hill Action Committee (a civic group) and sue the city collectively. The group called for better, more efficient use of the north-south runway to alleviate flights on the east-west runway. The gathering was also attended by FAA and airport officials, who said they were trying their best.

## General and Commercial Aviation— Problems Arise

In the early 1960s, more than 250 small aircraft were housed at Stapleton, and general aviation accounted for 51 percent of the field's air operations (that figure rose to 70 percent by 1967)—helping to maintain the airport's position among the top 15 airports in the country. But in 1963, it was reported that 60 percent of all pilots using Stapleton were still flying by the seat of their pants, with no instruments or flight plans, causing slowdowns, congestion and inefficiency on the busy runways.

Nationally, there were 80,000 general aviation planes in use, carrying each month three times as many passengers three times as many miles as the nation's 2,000 commercial aircraft. Late in 1961, the FAA recommended to Congress that 131 general aviation airports be built immediately to relieve congestion at 55 major city airports, including Stapleton. Congress appropriated $14 million to be used with matching funds from each region.

Denver officials stated, however, that the city could not act on this until 1966, at the earliest. The city, they said, had no money to match funds, and the self-liquidating bonds used for airport construction needed general aviation revenues to be retired on schedule. Although everyone admitted general aviation created a great deal of problems for Stapleton, no one was ready to throw this lucrative business off the field.

This realization of private plane worth did not, however, deter conflict between the airport and general aviation. In June 1961, it was reported that Stapleton had won a court case against J. S. Duff, who owned a private plane service just west of the airport. Stapleton had seized Duff's land for expansion, and the issue had gone to court. The court ruled that the airport had the legal right to acquire land for the announced purpose of expanded operations or safety control.

Although general aviation was a large segment of Stapleton's business, it did not proportionately pays its share of improvements. Denver officials, realizing general aviation was big business with small profits, expected the commercial airlines to foot the bill for most improvements through their landing fees.

At this time, Denver charged 9.52 cents per 1,000 pounds—New York charged 35 cents and San Francisco 20.1 cents—but wanted to raise that to 15 cents because commercial carrier fees comprised only 15 percent of airport revenues while maintenance of landing areas accounted for 46 percent of the airport's expenses. United and Continental, because of a 1940s contract, had to pay only 3 cents per 1,000 pounds, yet United had agreed to pay the 9.52 cents in a spirit of helping the airport. Continental was still paying the 3-cent charge.

With the suggestion that landing fees be raised to 15 cents, the commercial airlines felt they were being singled out to pay for improvements while there were airport concessions that should share the burden, too. United Airlines president, W. A. Patterson, felt that making only the airlines pay for improvements was "compartmentalizing" the airport, and that it was impossible to divorce the concession facilities from the rest of the airport. The *Rocky Mountain News,* June 10, 1961, quoted Patterson as saying, "It would be a mighty lonesome place without airplanes and runways at the airport."

*Mayor Currigan helped kick off the ceremonies that included precision flying by the Colorado National Guard, a fire department demonstration on emergency procedures and more during October 16 and 17, 1964. Courtesy of the Western History Department, Denver Public Library.*

Mayor Batterton responded, in the same article, by saying, "each major area must pay its own way," and that the city would not use concession revenues to underwrite deficits incurred in other airport areas.

In the midst of these discussions both United and Continental made corporate decisions that affected Stapleton's status as an important air center. In early 1962, United announced that approximately 350 personnel at Stapleton would be transferred to new facilities near O'Hare Airport, while maintaining about 1,700 at Stapleton. Later that year, Continental announced that it would be moving its executive headquarters in July 1963 from Stapleton to Los Angeles Airport, transferring about 300 employees. Both moves did not seriously affect airport revenues because actual flight operations were not reduced, but the moves were seen as blows to Stapleton's status as an important air center. Also, the moves were viewed by many as directly related to Denver's demands for increased landing fees, although that was never officially mentioned by United or Continental officials.

It was not until 1965, nearly four years later, that the airlines and the airport reached an agreement. In January, all eight carriers, including Continental and United, signed 12-year contracts for 15 cents per 1,000 pounds, to be renegotiated every three years. The long conflict that had really begun back in the 1950s was over.

Even with the fight over landing fees, the commercial airlines did not stop asking Denver to help them expand their operations at Stapleton. During the mid- to late 1960s, United, Frontier and Continental had facilities built for them by the city and financed through long-term leases and self-liquidating bonds. Denver voters, in August 1965, approved a $24 million bond issue to be specifically used to build airline facilities.

United's facility was a flight-training school located on the northeast corner of East Thirty-second and Quebec streets in front of the terminal. In 1943, United's Cheyenne flight-training school had been moved to Denver. But by the late 1960s, the airline wanted more modern facilities. United agreed to a 32-year lease at $44,201 a year—3.9 cents per square foot—in exchange for construction of the $7 million facility. By the time it was completed in August 1968, the total cost of the building was $30 million. This facility currently houses many different types and kinds of flight simulators by which pilots can experience extremely realistic situations, learning the best ways to handle aerial emergencies while still on the ground. The training center also teaches courses to pilots and flight crews from other major U.S. airlines and foreign airlines around the world.

The same bond arrangement that financed United's center also financed a $10 million Frontier hangar and office building complex as a maintenance and training

base, which was completed in April 1969. Continental, in June 1966, also asked Denver to build a general office building and hangar facility, located on a 21-acre site near the United and Frontier facilities. The ground breaking for this $7 million facility did not take place until May 1969, with completion in the early 1970s. The new Continental building housed a flight kitchen, maintenance and reservation office, and was capable of handling the new Boeing 747 jumbo jets, which first appeared in Denver in 1970.

During the constantly changing relationship between the airport and the airlines in the 1960s, one thing did make the airlines extremely happy: Denver's termination of James C. Buckley as airport consultant in June 1966. Buckley and the airlines had continually fought over expansion plans and landing fees since he first began working for Denver in 1949. Denver decided to fire Buckley, city officials stated, because he had been consistently slow with reports, citing a report asked for in 1963 that was still not in by June 1966. The consulting firm of Landrum & Brown of Ohio was hired to fill Buckley's position.

## Stapleton Airfield Gets a New Name

In 1964, the Denver Chamber of Commerce made a proposal to the Denver City Council that the name of Stapleton Airfield be changed to "Denver International Airport, Stapleton Airfield" during the airport's thirty-fifth anniversary ceremonies in October. The chamber explained that such a name change might speed up official international designation of the airport and could possibly attract actual direct international flights. At the time, Stapleton was connected internationally to Mexico and Canada, but only through connecting flights, not directly. It would not be until more than four years later that Denver officially became an international airport when, on December 1, 1968, a Western Airlines flight from Calgary, Alberta, Canada, came to Denver nonstop.

The council agreed, but modified the chamber's proposal to "Stapleton International Airport." The dedication ceremonies took place Saturday and Sunday, October 16 and 17. There were flybys by the Colorado National Guard, precision flying, displays of antique aircraft, performances by the Air Force Academy's Drum and Bugle Corps and a fire department demonstration of emergency procedures in case of an air crash.

Spectator areas were located at Syracuse Street and Smith Road, and Yosemite Street and Smith Road—gone were the days of allowing people onto the field to watch the show; the airport had grown too large. But there were short flights—similar to those offered in earlier years—around Denver by Braniff and Frontier for $3.25 a ticket. There was also an "old-timers" breakfast on

*On the 35th Anniversary of the airport in 1964 Mayor Thomas Currigan (1963-1968) revealed the airport's official new name — Stapleton International Airport. Courtesy of the Colorado Aviation Historical Society.*

*May 1965. Looking out from construction on the main terminal to concourse C. Courtesy of the Western History Department, Denver Public Library.*

The largest plane in the world. In the early 1960s, a converted DC-7 called the "Flying Guppie" flew in and out of Stapleton carrying Titan missile parts for Martin Marrietta. The plane was said to look like a balloon when it was flying, and it was discovered that its engines were inadequate for the plane's payload. Courtesy of the Colorado Aviation Historical Society.

In 1965-1966 construction had begun on the second story drive that would take people to their airline check-in counters. Courtesy of the Denver Post.

Sunday—Mrs. Helen (Mom) Williams, who had run the first airport restaurant from 1929 to 1934, was guest of honor. Another guest at the ceremonies was Arthur Godfrey, who had piloted his plane to Denver for the event.

During the dedication, Stapleton was also officially designated a Port of Entry, and plans were made to establish a customs and immigration office at the airport. This facility began operations on May 1, 1967, and was only open on weekdays to inspect international cargo. When Western Airlines' direct Canadian flight came into Stapleton, the customs and immigration office had newly expanded basement facilities on concourse C.

On its thirty-fifth birthday, Stapleton had grown from 640 acres to 3,864, and from a capital investment of $430,000 in 1929 to $45.7 million in 1964. More than 8.5 million passengers and visitors passed through Stapleton's doors in 1964, making it the fourth busiest airport in the country. There were eight commercial carriers located at the airport in 1964: United, Continental, Western, Braniff, Aspen Airways, Central Airlines, Frontier and TWA. Clinton and Combs, the two general aviation companies, were also there. Total flight operations in 1964 increased by 36 percent from the year before, boosting Stapleton's total operations ranking from seventeenth to seventh—meaning to Stapleton's controllers that 65–75 planes landed or took off during peak hours.

Although phase two of the master plan was not yet completed when Stapleton held its anniversary, three months after the celebration the two concourses, B and C (part of phase two), were finished. The airlines were assigned gates, and United unveiled its new "telescoping jetways" on concourse B. These jetways could be extended 55 feet and move laterally six feet from the concourse to an airplane. This was the first time at Stapleton that passengers could board an airplane without going outside.

## The Master Plan of the 1950s is Finally Completed

Phase one of the master plan of the 1950s had been completed in 1962, but it took four more years to complete phase two. The major portion of phase two was finished in March 1966 with the opening of the new terminal facilities, which were six times the size of the old terminal. Politicians, airport and airline officials attended a low-key celebration on April 1, 1966, with a breakfast and the raising of city, state and national flags at the airport.

The new terminal was four stories high and had taken $11 million and two years to complete. The first floor was for baggage claim, rental car and limousine

services. The third and fourth floors were for airport and airline office space. An elevated drive for departing passengers led to the terminal's second level where each airline had a door into the building—United had two doors because they accounted for almost half of the business at Stapleton. Upon passing through the doors, passengers would find airline ticket counters and, beyond these, the "Great Hall." In the Great Hall—that was "like entering a plush shopping center"—were the concessions: a newsstand, gift shop, novelty shop; stores that sold candy, western wear and oriental items; a hobby shop, barber shop, bank and game room. There were more than 2,000 telephones throughout the terminal that needed no switchboard but could be dialed in and out directly. The Sky Chefs Restaurant, also in the Great Hall, had been rebuilt and renamed Crossroads West because, as Oliver C. Berthoud of Sky Chefs said, Denver was the airlines' crossroads.

The three concourses, A, B, and C, were in different color schemes—A was green, B was blue and C was yellow and orange. Concourse A was for small commuter airlines and concourse B and C were for the major air carriers.

*The 14-story control tower commandeers a view never imagined by those who stood on the top of the original three-story terminal. Courtesy of the* Denver Post.

On April 30, 1967, when all projects in phase two were completed, an official celebration was held. The ceremonies were open to the public, with guided tours of all new facilities given by 70 former airline stewardesses. The dedication program included performances by the U.S. Air Force Academy band and the erection of a plaque on the second floor which read, "To the citizens of Denver, Colorado, and our visitors from all over the world, whom we welcome."

For the thousands who attended, it was a proud moment. Stapleton reflected a $56 million investment with its new terminal, seven hangars, a two-story 2,400-car parking lot, two major runways—the newly completed 11,500-foot north-south, and the 10,000-foot east-west—and one shorter, 5,700-foot east-west runway for general aviation, all on 3,978 acres. (The original 7,400 north-south runway directly in front of the terminal that had been used before the 11,500-foot north-south was built, became inoperative with the new concourses and expanded airport facilities.) There were then 11 commercial airlines operating from Stapleton: United, Continental, Western, Frontier, Braniff, TWA, Trans Central, Vail, Ozark, Aspen and Central. Stapleton, in 1967, ranked ninth in total takeoffs and landings with 442,220—a plane flying in or out every minute and 11 seconds—seventeenth in commercial airline operations (129,111) and fifth in general aviation activity (313,109).

## A New Master Plan Creates Controversy and Dispute

Even as the master plan of the 1950s was being completed in 1967, airport and city officials had begun working on a new plan. The necessity for the new plan came from the airport's increasing operations that were straining the new facilities to their limits as well as the developments in the late 1960s of the jumbo jet and Supersonic Transport (SST).

The jumbo jet, not seen on regularly scheduled flights at Stapleton until 1975, nonetheless posed a threat to the airport's runways and passenger facilities with its weight and runway length demands, and its increased passenger capacity. Because of the jumbo jet's greater passenger capacity, airport officials reasoned that when the jumbo jets came to Denver, Stapleton's passenger count could increase with no corresponding jump in total aircraft activity. This could make the airport's passenger facilities inadequate while not overburdening Stapleton's runways. The SST, while posing no such problems, did, however, create citizen protest over possible pollution and noise impact when, and if, the plane came to Denver.

The aviation activity at Stapleton during 1967, and the possibility of far greater activity in the near future, not

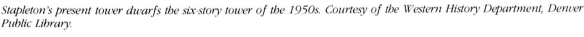

*Stapleton's present tower dwarfs the six-story tower of the 1950s. Courtesy of the Western History Department, Denver Public Library.*

*By May 1966 the check-in drive had been completed and seemed to surround the United building that had been built in 1953. Courtesy of the* Denver Post.

*In April 1966 the new four-story terminal was completed. It was six times the size of the old terminal and featured a "Great Hall," which was likened to a "plush shopping center." Courtesy of the* Denver Post.

only stimulated development of a new master plan, it also drove some business away from the airport. In 1967, Clinton Aviation, an important and large segment of Stapleton's general aviation business, made the decision to move its base of operations to the newly established Arapahoe Airport, which catered to private and small business aircraft. This move did hurt the airport somewhat financially, but it also relieved some of the congestion at Stapleton; total flight operation figures dropped when Clinton left and took years to regain their former numbers.

In March 1967, while Clinton was deciding on its move, a $100 million master plan to carry the airport through 1980, was announced. Although the official celebration for completion of the plan started in the 1950s was a month away, the new plan called for terminal expansion, a new concourse, a monorail system, more parking, strengthening and lengthening of the present runways, a second north-south runway, acquisition of Arsenal land and construction of a new airport terminal north of the present one after 1972.

The proposed terminal expansion, calling for almost doubling of the facility's size, would be to the north and be four stories high. This would mean one hangar would have to be destroyed and another moved to make room. Within the terminal a monorail system was planned to move passengers from the terminal to the

concourses and gates. The system would cost $300 per foot, as opposed to $700 per foot for moving walkways and be able to carry 50 passengers (28 seated) in six cars per concourse, giving the system the capacity of moving 8,000 people per hour.

As for the concourses, the plan called for giving concourse A a second story (B and C were two-story), and building a "Y"-shaped concourse D, which would have 25 gates. Other proposed construction included a third level parking lot for 500 cars, new aprons and taxiways for proposed new hangars, enlargement of the cargo building and a new Sky Chefs flight kitchen.

Runway proposals called for reconditioning and strengthening the present north-south and east-west runways to handle jumbo jets, and the building of a new 13,500-foot north-south runway in 1971. The new runway would be to the northeast of the present north-south and, obviously, require Arsenal land. As for acquisition of Arsenal land, the master plan outlined a two-phase program. The first phase was to get 415 acres and the second phase called for acquiring 10 parcels of Arsenal land totalling 6,500 acres.

The complete master plan received support from Denver and airport officials, airport consultants and the city council. What was needed was FAA approval. Once that was received, Denver would then have to go after the necessary Arsenal land by itself.

Before the FAA gave its approval to the master plan, however, Adams County officials reacted vehemently to the proposed land acquisition and new runway. In January 1968, Adams County commissioners said they would take Denver to court if it tried to expand the airport any more. The commissioners wrote a letter to Denver, state and federal officials stating that Denver wanted to expand because of the possibility of supersonic flights into Stapleton—which they opposed. The *Denver Post* on January 16, quoted the letter as stating, "[We] wish to go on record in vehement opposition to such acquisition [of Arsenal land] and use by . . . Denver." The letter gave two reasons for the commissioners' opposition: the growth of Adams County would be jeopardized and the effect of supersonic aircraft on the area. Adams County also wanted Arsenal land for its own expansion, and felt, because the Arsenal site was originally Adams County land, that it should have first crack at acquiring the land.

During the summer of 1968, Denver and Adams County decided to form a committee of six to resolve the dispute over Stapleton. But this time, however, Adams County did not just oppose Stapleton's expansion, it wanted the airport to move entirely. The county commissioners even offered to work with Denver on obtaining 25,000 acres of Adams County land east of Aurora for the new airport.

Meanwhile, it was discovered in February 1968, that the FAA was withholding approval of Stapleton's master

*Stapleton Airport by 1967 reflected a $56 million investment with a new terminal, seven hangars and three runways, all on 3,978 acres. Courtesy of the Colorado Historical Society.*

*Even with the newly completed terminal, plans were being formulated for more improvements. One of them was a monorail system to move people from the terminal to the concourses and gates. Courtesy of the* Denver Post.

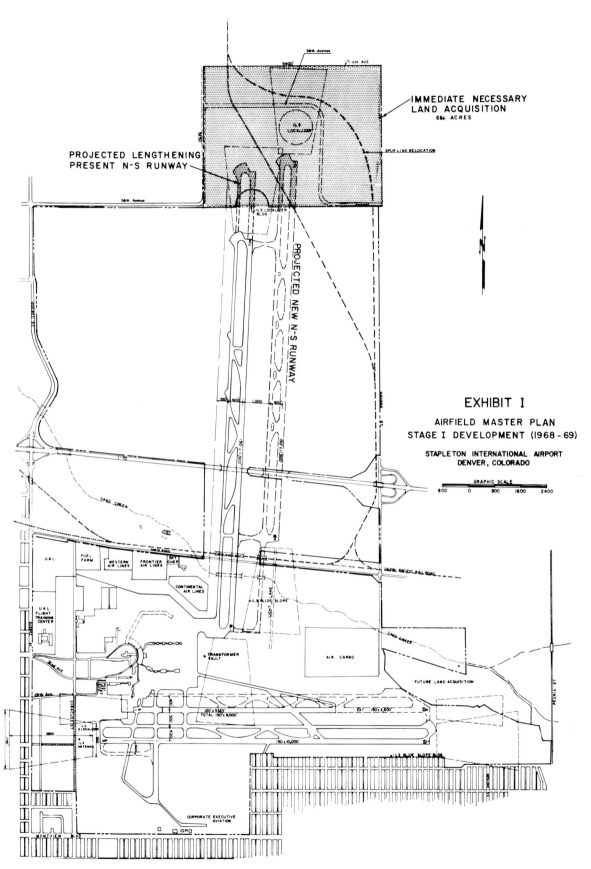

Part of the late 1960s planning for the airport included a new north-south runway and lengthening of the existing north-south runway. Both ideas relied on acquiring 651 acres of Rocky Mountain Arsenal land. Courtesy of Stapleton International Airport.

plan until it could be studied thoroughly. By May, the FAA had given its approval to master plan construction, but not to Arsenal land acquisition. William McNichols, then public works manager, was quoted by the *Denver Post* on May 8, 1968, as saying, "If we don't have approval of the arsenal land acquisition by January 1969, we would have to begin construction on a brand new airport at another site."

To further complicate the issue, the Army made a statement two days later that they could not afford to give up any land to Denver—or anyone else—because it was needed as buffer zones for production of classified materials.

On August 11, 1968, the *Denver Post* ran an article on Stapleton's master plan and reported that experts foresaw the need of another terminal north of the present one and three new runways—all on Arsenal land. They said that if that idea (similar to scheme E of the 1950s) could not be done, the airport would have to be moved. The newspaper, wondering if Stapleton would indeed have to move, asked the question of its readers: "Will Stapleton be ready for the million-pound, 1,000-passenger nuclear powered aircraft that may be in operation by 1990? And how about local rocket service to the moon? Why not? We're already a mile closer than most other parts of the nation."

Even with the talk about moving the airport and the Arsenal's reluctance to part with any land, city and airport officials, in 1968, revised their initial land request of 6,915 acres (415 acres and 10 parcels totally 6,500 acres) to a request for the Arsenal's entire 18,000 acres. This decision was based to a large degree on rumors circulating that the Arsenal would be removing its nerve gas and closing down in the near future. Denver did, however, say that it would start by officially requesting only 600 acres—the land necessary for the proposed 13,500-foot north-south runway.

Upon hearing of Denver's new plan, the Adams County commissioners once again reacted. They immediately formed a group, including many of the county's city mayors, and headed to Washington to make their opposition known.

At this point, the FAA returned to the forefront of the controversy by announcing a condition to its approval of the master plan. The FAA wrote Don Martin, airport manager, in November 1968 outlining the condition. The *Rocky Mountain News*, on November 15, ran an excerpt from the letter, "If either the transfer or notice of intent to transfer the required 6,500 acres of arsenal property is not obtained by January 1, 1969, the city will abandon the present plan and proceed immediately with planning for a new carrier airport."

The implications of that statement were staggering: If Denver could not get a promise from the Army within a month and a half, the city would have to scrap both its $100 million plan and its $56 million Stapleton Airport.

Don Martin immediately filed for an extension of the deadline to July 1, 1969, which he ultimately received. The FAA also wrote in the letter that Stapleton was to begin construction of a new north-south runway immediately. The city could not comply with this, however, because it still did not have the necessary 600 acres of Arsenal land.

As if this was not enough, in January 1969, Adams County commissioners drew up a resolution opposing the use of Arsenal land by Stapleton and sent a copy to the Army, FAA, Denver and state officials. The resolution again mentioned that Stapleton expansion would hurt Adams County's growth. The county also accused Denver of participating in the committee meetings to

*The first wedding at Stapleton was performed at the airport's chapel on New Year's Day 1969. Carol Bollinder and Ronald Goettsche were both employees of Western Airlines. Courtesy of the Western History Department, Denver Public Library.*

resolve the issue while never mentioning the continual changes it was making in the expansion plan.

By spring of 1969, while land and expansion issues were being debated, certain parts of the master plan, not dependent upon land acquisition, were either being started or completed. The terminal's northern expansion would begin, as would construction on concourse D. The concourse would be 1,700 feet and have 29 gates (up from the originally planned 25 gates). Concourses B and C would be widened and lengthened, while construction of a $1.5 million Sky Chefs building on Smith Road would begin in August. Also, construction was already underway on the Frontier, Western, United and Continental hangars south of Smith Road. Plans were also made to extend the

*In 1969 William McNichols became mayor of Denver. Throughout his administrations he has been a strong backer of the airport, due in part, to the fact that he had been manager of public works from 1963-1969 and understood the importance of the facility in Denver's future. Courtesy of the Western History Department, Denver Public Library.*

shorter east-west runway from 5,700 feet to 9,700 feet, and in June 1969, the major east-west runway was reconditioned in preparation for the new jumbo jets.

Even with Stapleton's construction, the Arsenal land problem was never far from the minds of airport officials. On March 19, 1969, a partial solution occurred. The army announced that Denver could have 651 acres to build a new north-south runway, if the city would pay the cost of relocating some buildings that would have to be moved when the runway was built. Denver agreed to the terms and received the deed for the land on November 24, 1969—but the deed was for only 622 acres, not the promised 651. Construction of the runway would begin in the spring of 1970, and many experts believed it would meet the traffic needs of the airport through 1981.

The traffic needs of the airport, however, were building at such a pace that it was difficult for the airport or the traffic controllers to keep up. Many controllers also felt that the federal government was not doing enough to help them ensure air safety. On June 18 and 19, air traffic controllers across the country staged a sick out and a slowdown as part of what they called "Operation Air Safety," in objection to the lack of safety emphasis in the Nixon administration's new airways program. To show how they had to skirt the rule book to handle the volume of air traffic, controllers across the country went strictly by the book on June 18 and 19, and the resulting delays in air travel proved their point. During the two days of protest, 7,200 of the 9,345 Professional Air Traffic Controllers Organization members (PATCO) reported in sick, 40 of which were in Denver. The controllers did not go on strike because they were government employees who, by signing their contracts, had given up the right to strike.

The June 1969 slowdown and sick out was not the first time this had happened. On August 14, 1968, the *Rocky Mountain News* reported: "Air traffic controllers have recently been accused of a slowdown of their operations. Some readily admit this, but insist that they are merely controlling by the Federal Aviation Administration book, in an effort to point up growing dissatisfaction with working conditions."

The *Rocky Mountain News* went to the control tower at Stapleton to view controllers first hand. The paper stated that controllers had "one of the most difficult, ulcerous and demanding jobs modern technology has managed to create."

Traffic controller protests would continue through the 1970s, finally coming to a head with the controversial walkout in the 1980s.

Even with the controllers slowdown in 1969, the citizen and county protests, the problems with the Arsenal and federal agencies, Stapleton ended the 1960s on a high note, for it had the land to build a new runway and nothing was going to stop the city from building it.

*On August 13, 1979 another important aircraft came to Denver — the space shuttle Enterprise on the back of a Boeing 747. It was being moved from Florida to California for tests. © 1979 Pat Olson.*

# Chapter Six

The 1970s were important, but turbulent, years for Stapleton, marked by a plethora of critical events and situations: traffic controller slowdowns, jumbo jets coming to Denver, continual evolution of growth and expansion plans, controversy and citizen protests over those plans, the facility's first experience with hijacking, implementation of tighter security measures, government deregulation of the airline industry, serious consideration toward relocating the airport, and appearances by the SST and the space shuttle, Enterprise.

At the start of the decade, traffic controllers once again began a nationwide protest against working conditions and FAA safety measures by staging sick outs and going strictly by the rule book—causing extensive flight delays. By the first part of April 1970, termination notices were sent out to some of the controllers who had participated in the protests. At Stapleton, almost half of the regular controller staff, 26 of 49, had called in sick during the protest, and supervisory and administrative personnel had been used to fill in for the protesters. On April 2, 1970, 15 Denver controllers received their termination notices, including the head of the local PATCO chapter, Gerald Phillips.

Throughout the 1970s, the air traffic controller situation only got worse, with federal officials and PATCO representatives never fully reaching accords that would appease both sides. It would not be until 1981 that a national walkout by most of the PATCO controllers would bring the issues to a dramatic conclusion.

## Jumbo Jets Come to Denver

At Stapleton, officials were confident that the $100 million master plan of the 1960s would properly prepare the airport for jumbo jets. Denver had received the 622 acres of Arsenal land necessary for the new jumbo jet north-south runway. Further, concourse D construction—that would give the airlines more gates—was under way, and terminal expansion plans were being reviewed.

During this optimistic time, the first jumbo jet touched down at Stapleton on November 18, 1970. The aircraft, a Continental Boeing 747, was carrying Continental officials from Los Angeles to Stapleton for the dedication of the $7 million "Robert F. Six Operations Center"—a hangar/office facility. After the ceremonies, the jet took a select group of Denver officials and media people on a champagne lunch flight to the Grand Canyon and back.

In March 1971, jumbo jets began flying regularly scheduled flights in and out of Stapleton. Although they could land on the 10,000-foot east-west runway, they could not land on the north-south, which had not been built to handle such loads. Even with one runway capable of supporting the jets, problems arose. In May, the *Denver Post* reported that one 747 had broken part of a runway shoulder off while turning around, and another had gone 100 feet off the end of a runway because it could not stop fast enough. The FAA had been monitoring jumbo jet activity at Stapleton during this time and ordered the airport to make certain repairs and improvements immediately.

The airport's improvement plans included grooving the runways to help the jets' stopping action during inclement weather, widening runway shoulders by 50 feet to conform to new FAA rulings, and lengthening the shorter east-west runway, which was used primarily by general aviation aircraft. Although the lengthening of the east-west runway would still not make it capable of handling jumbo jets, it was felt that with its new length it could help relieve normal jet congestion from Stapleton's primary runways.

By early 1972, it was announced that Stapleton would be closed to all jumbo jets for nearly 30 days so that these improvements could be made. It was not, however, until the fall that the airport was closed for the grooving and widening of runways (September 10–October 9); lengthening of the east-west runway was planned for spring 1973.

Jumbo jets not only caused problems for Stapleton and other airports, they also created difficulties for the airline industry in the early 1970s. The capital expenditures for the new jets, coupled with lagging ticket sales, hurt the financial position and proposed growth plans of many air carriers. In past years, the commercial airlines had experienced 12–15 percent nationwide growth rates, while the averages in the early

# From Denver Airfield 1929

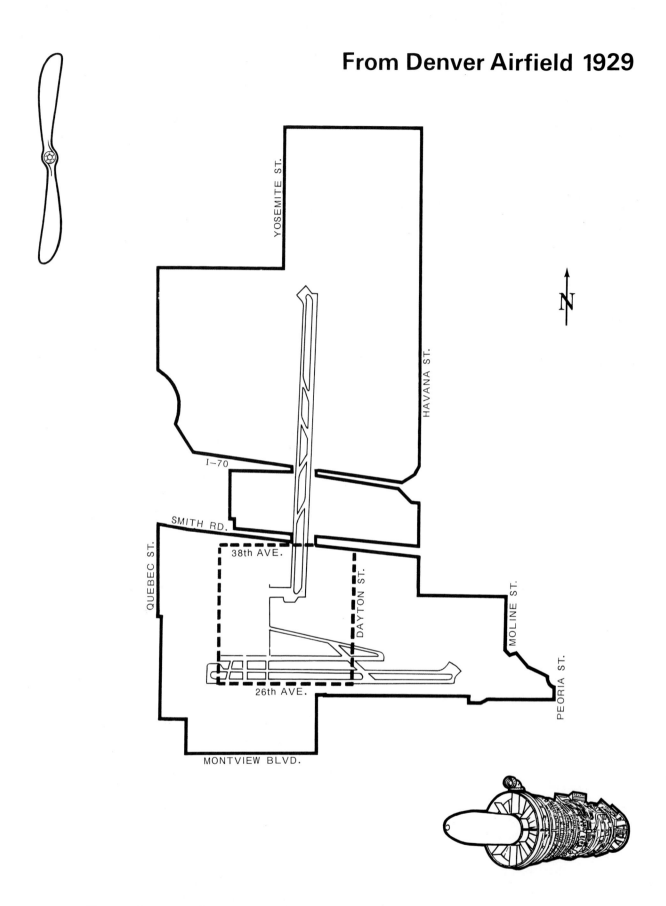

YOSEMITE ST.

HAVANA ST.

N

I–70

SMITH RD.

QUEBEC ST.

38th AVE.

DAYTON ST.

MOLINE ST.

PEORIA ST.

26th AVE.

MONTVIEW BLVD.

# ...to Stapleton International Airport 1970

◄ By 1970 the airport had grown substantially from the 640 acres originally purchased in 1929. Courtesy of Stapleton International Airport.

Every year drills are run by the fire department and other emergency services to test the readiness of Denver in case of a major air crash. Volunteers help out by pretending to be victims. Courtesy of the Federal Aviation Administration.

1970s were only 2–3 percent. Most airports were following similar declining growth patterns. Stapleton, because of its central location nationally had become a crossroads airport and, thus, was not hurt as badly as other airports. In the first two years of the 1970s, it had an average 6 percent increase in activity, and would continue to buck the trend for the next few years.

Stapleton's good fortune, however, did create problems for the master plan. Because of the airport's growth rate, city and airport officials were still in favor of the plan, while the airlines—who would ultimately be paying for expansion with landing fees and rents—had become understandably reluctant to back the entire proposal. The airline companies' lack of growth, therefore, became a major factor in the decision to scrap the master plan's outline of building a separate terminal and three new runways on Arsenal land by 1981.

Even with the cutback in the master plan, there was still discussion about the possible need to relocate the airport. In mid-1971, it was announced that the Denver Regional Council of Governments (DRCOG), representing 30 municipalities and 5 counties, would be conducting a federally funded study of Stapleton. The group would determine validity of the master plan, whether or not the airport should be moved, and if moved, where, and what part the Arsenal would play in Stapleton's future. Although Adams County was represented on DRCOG, the Adams County Planning Commission felt the need to submit a position paper to DRCOG stating the airport should be moved to an eastern location, not expanded on its present site. The *Denver Post* ran an excerpt from the paper on August 4, 1971, "There is no rational basis for an assumption that airports, regardless of size, location or the pattern of surrounding land uses, should be expanded indefinitely at the expense of environmental quality for residents of the adjacent communities."

## Stapleton's New Jumbo Jet Runway

By August 1971, DRCOG had reviewed Stapleton's plan for the proposed $17.5 million north-south jumbo jet runway and approved its application for federal funds. Next, the airport's application went to the Colorado State Planning Commission and then to the U.S. Department of Transportation for final approval. The application described the runway as 12,000 feet long and the location as being 1,600 feet east of the existing north-south runway. Ultimately, approval from all agencies was granted, and the government paid for almost half of the project.

When PATCO learned of the runway's specifics, it strongly suggested the proposed 1,600 feet separating the two runways be extended to 3,500 feet. This way PATCO explained, FAA requirements on distance between parallel runways during instrument flights could be met. FAA rules stated that during bad weather when instrument landings and take offs became necessary, parallel runways that were not 3,500 feet apart could not be fully utilized, for fear of accidents. Don Martin, director of the airport, responded to PATCO's suggestion by stating it simply could not be done because the city did not have the necessary land for greater runway separation.

Another suggestion for the runway was made in January 1971, when the city of Aurora proposed to the Denver City Council that the new runway be started north of I-70. Aurora explained that if the runway was moved further north there would be fewer Aurora citizen complaints, and Denver would be saved the cost of building an overpass across I-70. The city council approved the plan, and the proposed runway was moved north.

In May 1972, the FAA granted approval for the jumbo jet runway and work was begun immediately. Although the I-70 overpass had been dropped from the plans, overpasses across the union Pacific railroad tracks and Sand Creek were still needed. These structures were expected to cost $3 million and take a year to complete. But, while preparation work was going on, the Army once again began causing problems.

In May 1973, the Pentagon sent a letter to Mayor McNichols stating that it would not allow any more flying over Arsenal land, including future flights utilizing the proposed north-south runway, because of the storage of nerve gas at the Arsenal. Prior to this time, there had been certain restrictions on flight patterns over the Arsenal, but the letter from the Pentagon ordered a complete ban on all aircraft flying over the area. Robert S. Michael, director of the airport, was quoted in the *Denver Post* on May 24, as saying the Pentagon's statement put "[our] backs against the wall," and that "we are tremendously shocked and disappointed. The future of Denver's air transportation facilities is at stake here." Both Michael and Mayor McNichols flew to Washington to attempt to reverse the Army's new policy.

Many city and airport officials felt that the safety reasons given for the new restrictions were bogus claims and the real reasons for the new policy were political. When the city had received the 622 acres of Arsenal land for the new runway in 1969, it was agreed between the city and the commandant of the Arsenal that Denver would build $1.4 million worth of facilities at the Arsenal. The northern boundary of the deeded land was only 20 feet from the commandant's house, so the city had agreed to build a $125,000 house somewhere else, as well as a $170,000 officers club and some barracks. This plan had been accepted by all parties when the runway was to begin south of I-70.

City and airport officials believed the problems with

116

*Work was begun in the early 1970s on the new north-south runway. In this high altitude shot taken in 1976, the new runway is outlined. Courtesy of Stapleton International Airport, Colorado Aerial Photo Service.*

117

*On December 13, 1978 a Braniff Concorde Supersonic Transport landed at Stapleton. It was on a tour of 16 U.S. cities. © 1979 Pat Olson.*

the Army had begun when the proposed runway was moved further north, beyond I-70. The move meant that the runway would end right at the northern border of the deeded land and, therefore, have no buffer zone between it and the Arsenal for approach lights, landing aids and airspace. Denver had then asked, in early 1972, for an additional 480 acres to be used only for airspace and runway equipment.

At the same time the Pentagon sent the letter to Mayor McNichols in May 1973, Lieutenant Colonel Gerald G. Watson, commandant of the Arsenal—but not the same commandant who had initially worked with Denver on the runway—accused the city of not discussing the runway move with Arsenal officials. The move had been made, the Army said in the *Denver Post*, July 15, 1973, under "unorthodox procedures and secrecy." Denver officials responded to Watson by stating the city had, back in 1972, notified all the proper agencies of the move as well as the previous commandant.

What had in fact happened, was that Denver and the FAA had not informed the Pentagon or the Arsenal in an official letter. This had made the Army mad at both Denver and the FAA, so that when the FAA asked for airspace rights (easement rights) over the Arsenal and the right to place equipment on Arsenal land north of the runway, the Army had said no. Many in Denver felt

this response had been generated more from a sense of getting even rather than actual safety concerns.

Whatever the motivation, on June 28, 1973, the Arsenal made a stronger stand, stating there would be no new north-south runway until its nerve gas was significantly reduced, mentioning that this could take a long time due to Congress' strict control in moving chemical weapons cross-country.

Mayor McNichols was getting increasingly frustrated with the Arsenal's policies because the two overpasses were finished and bids had already come in for grading the runway. He felt that if he did not sign a grading contract soon, bids would have to be taken again and the prices would inevitably be higher. But if he signed the contract and then the airport could not use the runway, the action might have serious political consequences.

Before Mayor McNichols had to make such a decision, the Army wrote to him, in July 1973, stating easement rights might be granted by the summer of 1976. As reason for this, the Army cited a new three-year program to destroy the nerve gas. With this somewhat indirect promise, Mayor McNichols went ahead and signed a $5,498,183 grading contract.

By the end of 1975, the north-south runway was complete. It had taken $31 million to build, $13.5

On August 13, 1979 another important aircraft came to Denver — the space shuttle Enterprise on the back of a Boeing 747. It was being moved from Florida to California for tests. © 1979 Pat Olson.

million more than the original estimates. The new runway, 1,600 feet northeast of the old north-south runway, was 200 feet wide with 25-foot shoulders, and had 18 inches of concrete at its thickest point to handle the weight of the jumbo jets. Although no official easement had been given, airport and city officials boldly stated that the runway would be used with or without federal permission to fly over the Arsenal. Shortly after this, the government did give its permission.

The future of Stapleton had relied heavily on the new runway, and it was only through the perseverance of airport officials, Denver and state officials that Stapleton got its new runway. Experts had said that with the new runway, Stapleton's runway needs would be met until 1990. Somewhat ironically, with the opening of the new runway, it was announced that the old north-south runway would be closed for a year to a year and a half for resurfacing—the airport was right back to only two major runways.

## Terminal Construction Moves Ahead in the Early 1970s

Although much time during the early 1970s was devoted to solving the runway dilemma, officials were also aware that Stapleton needed improved and expanded passenger facilities. By the end of 1971, facility expansion was 80 percent complete, with a total estimated cost of $9 million. The expansion included a four-story, 425-foot section attached to the north side of the terminal, construction of a third-level parking lot, extension of the baggage claim area—five new carousels were added to make a total of nine—and a medical clinic. When the terminal section was completed in mid-1972, it nearly doubled the size of the building. Concourse D, completed in early 1972, was a quarter of a mile long and in a dog-leg shape, with moving walkways down its center—the monorail idea had been dropped.

By the end of 1972, the airport was doing well. There were 15 airlines operating from its facilities: six trunk carriers, four regional carriers, two third-level airlines and three intrastate airlines. The trunk carriers were Braniff, Continental, Mexicana, TWA, United and Western. The regional carriers were Frontier, North Central, Ozark and Texas International. The third-level carriers were Air Midwest and Trans Nebraska. The intrastate carriers were Aspen Airways, Rocky Mountain Airways and S. I. Airways. The extension of the shorter east-west runway was complete, and under the "preferential runway system" in use for years, 85 percent of all landings were from the east and 90 percent of takeoffs were to the north to accommodate the surrounding residential areas. As far as the airport's impact on the area, Stapleton supplied jobs to 6,200

people (as opposed to the 40 back in 1929), housed 250 general aviation aircraft—many owned by local citizens and businesses—and, reportedly, contributed directly and indirectly $150 million a year to the Denver area.

Even with these impressive figures, Stapleton did not make everyone happy. In 1971, the airport was the stage for a demonstration, protesting the hiring practices of construction firms working at Stapleton. The demonstrators felt the firms were not hiring enough minorities, and to capture attention, a group of them walked down the north-south runway. They demanded a halt of all air traffic and construction at Stapleton, threatening to blow up the airport's fuel depot and a 707 if it was not done. The runway was closed for 10–15 minutes while police cleared the people away, arresting 25 of them in the process.

Also in 1971, Park Hill residents once again gathered to discuss Stapleton's jet noise and flights over their area. On the evening of October 28, a meeting was held at the Park Hill Congregational Church between Park Hill residents and Robert R. Stapp, public affairs manager for Stapleton. Stapp explained that Park Hill was affected by only 15 percent of Stapleton's takeoffs and landings. But, the Park Hill people pointed out, all the jumbo jets were using the east-west runway, which meant flying over their area. Stapp responded by stating that the north-south runway could not handle the jumbo jets, but with completion of the new jumbo jet north-south runway jumbos would begin using it and the problem, for the most part, would be resolved. The people had trouble accepting this, however, because they had heard the same type of argument in the 1960s when jets had first come to Stapleton and officials had said that the then new north-south jet runway would take care of jets on the east-west runway. When that runway had been completed, however, Park Hill residents had reported no significant difference in noise or frequency of flights over their area. During the October 28 meeting, along with the arguments there was a great deal of laughter as six jets roared overhead while Stapp was speaking.

In November 1973, the Denver Regional Council of Governments completed the study they had begun in 1971. The San Francisco firm of Peat, Marwick, Mitchell & Co., working with the Denver firm of Meurer, Serafini & Meurer, Inc., had compiled the material for the DRCOG.

The study suggested three courses of possible action in handling Stapleton's future needs: expand Stapleton at its present location, build a new airport on Arsenal land or relocate the facility (no specific sites were recommended). The consultants did not, at the time, back any one alternative but did state that whatever choice was made, it should be acted on immediately because it would take 6 to 12 years to complete any of the three choices. The cost of construction varied with the three alternatives. Expanding Stapleton was estimated at $165 million–$203 million, while building either an airport on Arsenal land or relocating would cost $615 million.

On November 12, 1973, the first of numerous public hearings to gauge public reaction, was held at the Jefferson County Court House. At the meeting, the consultants presented their projections on Stapleton's growth. In 1970, they stated, 1.9 million people had begun trips from Stapleton; by the year 2000 the figure would be 19 million. The figure for all passengers using the airport—boarding, deplaning and transferring—would jump from 1970's 3.5 million to 35 million by 2000. Commercial takeoffs and landings, numbering 212,000 in 1972, would reach 600,000 by 2000, far exceeding Stapleton's reported capacity of 450,000.

The audience, composed primarily of residents living around Stapleton, supported either moving the airport as far away as possible or doing nothing to the facility. They rejected the suggestions of moving onto Arsenal land or further expansion at the present location. The consultants explained that they had ruled out the "do nothing" policy as infeasible if Stapleton was to remain an important regional and national airport.

Two months after the first public hearing, Peat, Marwick, Mitchell & Co. did back one of their alternatives, recommending to the DRCOG that Stapleton should stay where it was and simply expand. They cited the almost impossible task of obtaining Arsenal land and the extremely high cost of relocating the airport as primary reasons for discarding the two other alternatives. But a master plan for expansion, they felt, should be begun immediately. The consultants believed the runways (including the new north-south then under construction) would be able to handle Stapleton's needs through the year 2000, but the passenger facilities would need to be expanded. They also suggested that the general aviation airports at Longmont, Boulder, Arapahoe County and Jefferson County should be expanded and four new general aviation airports be built by 2000 to relieve congestion at Stapleton.

The strong recommendation to expand Stapleton brought a new wave of citizen protest, which was vented at another public hearing in March 1974. John R. Morris, Jr., associate professor at Colorado University's Denver Center and vice chairman of the Greater Park Hill Committee, was outspoken in his views about

*In 1979 Stapleton Airport celebrated its 50th anniversary with an "old Timers'" breakfast, the official opening of the Colorado Aviation Historical Museum on the third floor, and the dedication of the Carl Hummel Park in front of the terminal for the long-time groundskeeper who had retired. © 1979 Pat Olson.*

expanding Stapleton as opposed to constructing a new airport. The *Denver Post* quoted Morris at the meeting on March 7: "It is bad enough that you propose to retain 30,000 residents inside the unacceptable (NEF-30) noise contour for another 30 years, but it is absolutely incredible that we keep three schools in the airport glide path."

Most residents living around the airport favored the complete relocation of the airport because they felt the other two alternatives of expanding the present facilities or moving on to the Arsenal would cause pollution, noise and safety problems. The Denver Chamber of Commerce, while backing expansion of Stapleton, did, however, make a statement saying Stapleton had a finite existence and that it would be ultimately necessary to decide on a site for a new airport. The Sierra Club also backed the expansion of the present facilities because it felt there would be less environmental impact with that course of action than with relocation.

## New Safety Measures and Equipment Come to Stapleton

Much of the citizen protest over Stapleton was generated by what was felt to be unsafe conditions caused by flight patterns over residential areas. Although airport officials were doing their best to keep aircraft from flying over houses, there was not much more they could do, given Stapleton's congested air lanes and lack of space for more runways.

But if new runways could not be built, technology might be utilized to make better, more efficient use of existing runways and air lanes to improve air safety and possibly reduce the number of flights over residential areas. This was the FAA's goal through the 1970s, as it introduced advanced equipment at Stapleton.

At the end of 1971, Stapleton was the second airport in the country—after O'Hare—to receive the FAA's new Automated Radar Terminal System (ARTSIII). The ARTSIII could keep track of a plane's speed, course and altitude by "tagging" it with numbers, letters and symbols that were flashed on the controller's radar screen. Before the new system was installed, a controller had to mentally keep track of identification and physically record a plane's flight data—duties that jeopardized complete concentration and control of air traffic.

By the end of 1976, the FAA had two more systems ready for installation: the Minimum Altitude Safety Warning System, and the Category IIIA Instrument Landing System. The altitude system, covering a 64-mile radius, automatically warned radar personnel if a plane was flying too low for local terrain and obstacles like buildings or towers. The instrument landing system reduced the forward visibility necessary for inclement

weather landings—when instruments were used—from 1,800 feet to 700 feet. Stapleton was the first airport in the country to have both systems installed.

In March 1977, the FAA announced a new method for traffic control that could reduce jet noise and help avoid the stacking up of planes during peak hours, which was frequently responsible for aircraft circling over residential areas. The method, called Metering, Spacing and Profile Descent, was actually operated from the Longmont control center, not from Stapleton's tower. By controlling the speed of a plane through radio communication, a Longmont controller could have a craft reach one of the "metering fixes"—located northeast, southeast, southwest and northwest of Stapleton—at a specific time so that it could follow a predetermined glide path into Stapleton, arriving at a set time. Every day controllers at Longmont decided how many planes could be safely handled in an hour (the ideal was one plane per minute) through studying weather conditions and other variables, then worked backwards from the number determined to the metering fixed points and incoming planes. This way, they could give an incoming plane a specific speed to have it reach the fixed point at the right time. Supposedly, jet noise was reduced by the speed control and glide paths, and stacking was reduced by having planes arrive at Stapleton at controlled times. Some Stapleton controllers did say, however, that the system did not work as well in practice as in theory.

## Air Crashes at Stapleton During the 1970s

Although air safety was constantly being improved through the FAA's introduction of new equipment and methods, these measures could not completely prevent air accidents.

The first commercial airline accident at Stapleton in the 1970s was the crash of an American Airlines 707 on March 5, 1973. The four-engine jet had safely landed in Denver with one engine out, and a three-man crew had come from Tulsa to fly it back to base for repairs. Although one engine was out, the jet could be flown safely on three engines. On takeoff, however, a second engine failed, and the plane crashed back down on the runway. The 707 missed the I-70 bridge railing by only 100 feet before the left engine was sheared off and the plane burst into flames. Fortunately, the three crew members escaped with no injury through the copilot's window.

On Thursday, August 7, 1975, a Continental Boeing 727, with 124 passengers and seven crew aboard, rose off the ground for only a few moments before dropping back onto the runway. Passengers and crew escaped unharmed and the plane was sprayed with foam as a precaution against fire. The cause of the crash was attributed to a "wind shear" condition—a scissorslike movement of air layers blowing in opposite directions.

Only six days later, 40 representatives of Denver's various disaster units met to discuss the crash and what could have been done to improve their performance. Crash and emergency units were constantly trying to upgrade themselves, staging mock crashes every year to familiarize the crews with emergency procedures. During the 1970s, the FAA began requiring airport firemen to take a week long course in fighting jet fires and crashes.

On November 16, 1976, a Texas International DC-9, carrying 85 passengers, crashed on takeoff and caught fire. The pilot had decided to abort when a stall warning light—indicating loss of speed—had gone on. On landing, though, the plane overshot the east end of the major east-west runway and caught fire. Everyone escaped and only 12 had minor injuries, but the left side of the plane, where the fire had been concentrated, was totally destroyed.

Through the efforts and quick thinking of the pilots, flight crews and Stapleton firemen, no major disaster like the one in 1961 happened in the 1970s. An important factor in helping firemen respond to airport emergencies was the construction of a "satellite" fire station north of the terminal. The structure, which became operational in January 1977, cost $650,000 and was built because the old fire station—still in operation—could not meet the FAA's requirements for runway response time. The FAA stated that within three minutes of an alarm the first fire truck had to be able to reach the middle of the farthest runway, the second truck within four minutes and the remaining equipment in four and a half minutes. Because of the new north-south runway's northeast location, the old fire station's equipment could not meet those requirements, so a satellite station had to be built closer to that runway. Response time for the new station's three trucks to the runway was two minutes. The satellite fire station housed 10 men—4 on duty at a time—which brought the total of firemen stationed at Stapleton up to 42.

## Airport Security Measures Come to Denver

Air safety did not, however, cover only firefighting and FAA equipment for controllers: There was a growing threat, in the 1970s, of hijacking through smuggling of firearms and other weapons aboard aircraft.

On the national scene, incidents of hijacking and bomb threats were becoming alarmingly prevalent. On the night of October 9, 1970, the FAA received telephone bomb threats—credited to the Weatherman group—for numerous airports around the country. After carefully checking every facility named in the coast-to-coast threat, FAA sent bulletins to all airports and airlines in the United States, demanding greater security measures. Although Stapleton was not one of the airports threatened, officials realized that for the safety of all Stapleton air travelers tight security measures had to be adopted.

Shortly after the bomb threat, Denver city and airport officials met with airline executives and FAA personnel to discuss what needed to be done. Out of the meeting came the decision to close the airport's observation deck, lock all perimeter fences, and increase the number of perimeter checks by guards. No additional personnel were added to the airport's security force, but the airlines did decide to share the cost of placing guards around the fuel depot, and some air carriers began giving their personnel name badges to be worn in certain areas and hiring guards to protect their own facilities.

In early 1972, the FAA called for all scheduled airlines to screen every passenger boarding a plane. The screening of passengers had been done sporadically for the past two years by many of the airlines at Stapleton. The FAA's new regulation listed four screening methods that had to be implemented in three days, either individually or together. The first method was a hijacker behavioral profile, outlining certain actions and appearances that most hijackers exhibited. No details of this profile were released to the press for fear hijackers would learn how to mask these behavioral patterns. The second method was to use magnetometers or other metal detecting devices; the third to establish identification systems; and fourth to physically search passengers and baggage.

Most of the airlines chose to utilize the hijacker profile and spot searches until metal detecting equipment could be brought in. By July of 1972, four airlines—Continental, Western, United and TWA—were voluntarily searching every carryon item on flights out of Denver. City, airport and airline officials also decided, in 1972, that Denver policemen would be stationed around the clock in the airport lobby.

Anti-hijacking became the theme of 1972, when it was reported that nationally from July 1, 1969, to June 2, 1972, there had been 95 hijackings, of which 80 could have been prevented by more stringent security measures. In August 1972, the FAA gave Stapleton and 20 other airports new detection devices to screen baggage for explosives. Also, dogs were trained and put to use at Stapleton for guard work as well as for detection of explosives. Six months later, there were 12 Denver policemen working at the airport, with 13 more added the next month. By the beginning of 1973, all people going down any of the concourses were checked first, under the new "sterile" concourse

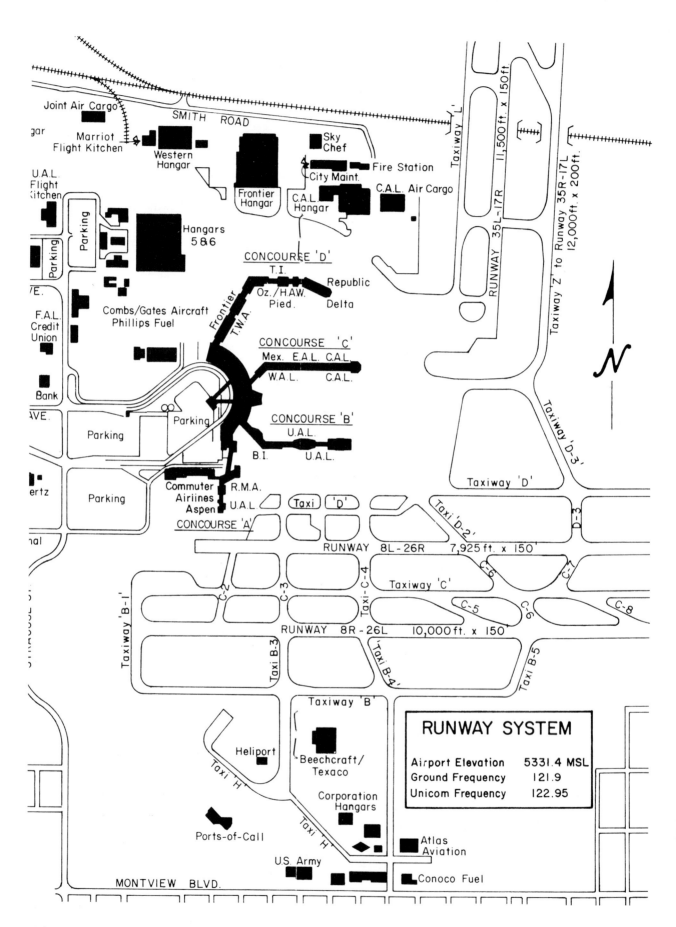

SMITH ROAD

Joint Air Cargo

Marriot
Flight Kitchen

Western
Hangar

Frontier
Hangar

Sky
Chef

City Maint.

Fire Station

C.A.L.
Hangar

C.A.L. Air Cargo

U.A.L.
Flight
Kitchen

Parking

Parking

Hangars
5 & 6

F.A.L.
Credit
Union

Combs/Gates Aircraft
Phillips Fuel

CONCOURSE 'D'

T.I.

Frontier

T.W.A.

Oz./H.A.W.
Pied.

Republic

Delta

Bank

CONCOURSE 'C'

Mex. E.A.L. C.A.L.

W.A.L.

C.A.L.

AVE.

Parking

Parking

Parking

Commuter
Airlines
Aspen

U.A.L.

CONCOURSE 'B'

U.A.L.

B.I.

U.A.L.

R.M.A.

Taxi 'D'

CONCOURSE 'A'

hal

Hertz

RUNWAY 8L - 26R     7,925 ft. x 150'

Taxi-C-4

Taxi 'D-2'

Taxi 'D-3'

Taxiway 'D'

Taxiway 'B-1'

Taxi B-3

Taxi 'C-3'

Taxi 'C-2'

Taxiway 'C'

RUNWAY 8R - 26L     10,000 ft. x 150'

'Taxi B-4'

Taxi B-5

C-5

C-6

C-8

C-3

Taxiway 'B'

Heliport

Beechcraft/
Texaco

Taxi 'H'

Taxi 'H'

Corporation
Hangars

Ports-of-Call

U.S. Army

Atlas
Aviation

Conoco Fuel

MONTVIEW BLVD.

Taxiway 'L'

RUNWAY 35L-17R     11,500 ft. x 150ft

Taxiway 'Z' to Runway 35R-17L
12,000ft. x 200ft.

RUNWAY 35R-17L

N

| RUNWAY SYSTEM | |
|---|---|
| Airport Elevation | 5331.4 MSL |
| Ground Frequency | 121.9 |
| Unicom Frequency | 122.95 |

*Stapleton International Airport — the fourth floor is office space. Courtesy of Stapleton International Airport.* ►

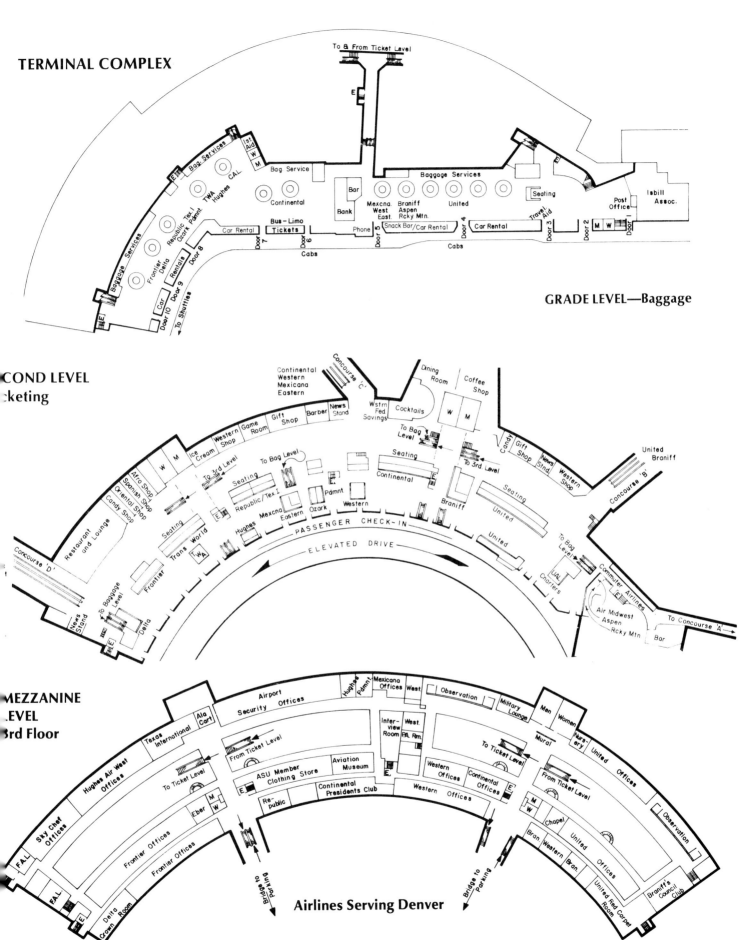

**TERMINAL COMPLEX**

**GRADE LEVEL—Baggage**

**SECOND LEVEL Ticketing**

**MEZZANINE LEVEL 3rd Floor**

**Airlines Serving Denver**

Air Midwest - Aspen - Braniff International - Continental - Delta - Eastern - Frontier - Hughes Airwest - Mexicana - Ozark - Piedmont - Republic - Texas International - Trans World - United - Western. **Commuters:** Air U.S. - Colorado Airlines - Pioneer Airways - Rocky Mountain - Shavano Air - Star Aviation - Sterling Air Service - Valley Airpark.

concept. By August 1973, there were a total of 28 Denver police officers at the airport, but the actual checking of people and baggage was done by two private security firms.

The firms reported that the average number of declared and undeclared weapons found in one month were 60–80 guns and 150–180 knives. By the end of 1973, the security firms had confiscated 342 knives, 44 guns and 234 explosives; had arrested 104 people; and denied boarding to 94 others. Of the 104 arrested, 85 were found to have made false threats, usually as a joke.

But all of these security measures and additional personnel could not completely protect Stapleton from hijacking. On Sunday, April 18, 1976, Roger L. Lentz, 31, of Grand Island, Nebraska, hijacked a twin-engine Piper Apache in Nebraska and, with two hostages, flew to Stapleton. He landed at 6:30 P.M. and demanded a jet to take him to Mexico. Twice he had the pilot take the small plane aloft, only to return again to Stapleton. The Denver police and FBI were called in and both Governor Lamm and Mayor McNichols were present.

After numerous attempts at negotiation failed, a Convair 900 jet was brought around for Lentz. Unknown to the hijacker, five FBI agents were waiting in the Convair. Lentz, with his two hostages, boarded the Convair, at 12:10 A.M.—at 12:13 A.M. Lentz was pronounced dead after a shoot-out with the FBI. Miraculously, the two hostages were unharmed. Stapleton had experienced its first hijacking.

Another tragedy occurred at Stapleton in November 1976, when Steven Killan, a 31-year-old ramp station attendant, was shot and killed when a loaded 357 magnum revolver in a duffel bag accidently discharged.

These two cases brought home to Denver citizens and airport officials what it was like when security was breached. Many people at Stapleton never again questioned the need for security measures taken at the airport.

## Lighter Moments at Stapleton

There were less serious moments at Stapleton during the 1970s. On December 6, 1973, the *Denver Post* reported that the National Organization of Women (NOW) had conducted a toilet survey at Stapleton in October and discovered out of the 125 pay toilets in the airport's 34 restrooms, 89 were for women and only 36 were for men. The survey—conducted by George and Jo Gorsuch, Lynn Brown and four children, Wendy Brown, Nora Spahn, Shannon and Danny Skaife—proved, NOW stated, sexual discrimination. The *Denver Post* reported airport business manager Bob Lowell's comment: "'Who let them in the men's room?' asked Lowell when informed of the survey. Then, on hearing

the results, he protested that, 'they're counting the urinals as freebies.'"

Lowell mentioned that the latest figures available on the pay toilets—from 1962—showed the airport had made $38,840 from the toilets in question. He also said that the situation could not be rectified until 1976 when the contract with the toilet concessionaire expired, because there was no cancellation clause written into the contract. Nothing was ever found by this author as to whether action was taken to change the situation or not.

The 1970s was also the decade when the International Society for Krishna Consciousness, better known as the Hare Krishnas, began appearing at Stapleton, soliciting funds from many unsuspecting arriving and departing passengers. They first appeared in 1972, chanting, handing out magazines, and soliciting throughout the terminal. By the fall of that year, the Denver City Council and airport officials had received enough complaints about the group that it was felt something should be done. The council, after realizing there was no legal way they could bar the group from the airport, passed two ordinances restricting the Krishnas' solicitation. The ordinances stated that the group had to apply for permits, stay within five feet of their booth and only solicit two weeks out of the year. The Krishnas challenged the ordinances in Denver's district court and won the right to solicit at will after obtaining a permit from the city and the airport.

This court action did not, however, deter private citizens and religious organizations from taking action. On August 6, 1979, Mitch Egan of San Francisco, founder of the Fellowship to Resist Organized Groups Involved in Exploitation (FROGIE) came to Stapleton. He distributed "clickers," small plastic devices that made loud clicking sounds, to anyone who would take them and suggested they be used if a member of the Hare Krishnas approached.

Also, in 1979, the Lovingway Inter-City United Pentecostal Church began a program to counteract the Krishnas' solicitation. Members of Lovingway, dressed in black suits and known as the "Truth Squad," began diverting people away from the Krishnas through talking, singing, yelling and sign waving. The Krishna organization filed charges against Lovingway, from which an agreement was reached that Lovingway members had to stay 10 feet away from any Krishna. This did not resolve the issue, for Lovingway members began carrying 10-foot poles around the airport bearing anti-Krishna signs. By late 1970, another agreement had been reached between the two groups—Lovingway would stay clear of the Krishnas as long as the Krishnas did not provoke them to action.

Today, the Krishnas still solicit at the airport, but the public address system continually announces that any group soliciting is not sanctioned by the airport authorities.

*Stapleton International Airport.* © *1979 Pat Olson.*

Another lighter moment during the 1970s was the arrival of a Braniff Concorde Supersonic Transport at Stapleton. On Tuesday, December 12, 1978, the SST, on a tour of 16 U.S. cities, flew into Denver at subsonic speed—supersonic speeds had been banned by the federal government over land. The craft was 204 feet long, 40 feet high, had a wingspan of 84 feet, seated 100 passengers and cost $88 million to build—twice the cost of a Boeing 747. It had four engines, could travel at 1,350 miles per hour, and cruised at an altitude of 50,000–60,000 feet.

During the short time it was parked at Stapleton, a select group of politicians, airport and airline officials and media people were allowed to get a closer look. Dwarfed by surrounding jets, yet exhibiting graceful lines, elegant swept-back wings and down-slanted nose, many found it difficult to believe that it had caused such controversy over noise and pollution. However, a KOA-TV acoustical engineer had set up equipment to register the plane's noise level as it landed, and found the SST to be eight times as loud as a normal jet. A sizeable crowd had come to gaze at the craft, for it had been reported this would probably be the only time an SST came to Denver—in October 1977 the city council passed a resolution opposing any supersonic flights at Stapleton.

Another aircraft that caused a stir when it came to Denver was the space shuttle, Enterprise, perched upon the back of a Boeing 747. At midday on August 13, 1979, thousands lined the airport's border fences trying to catch a glimpse of the two aircraft as they flew into Stapleton. The shuttle was being moved from Florida to California for tests, while its sister ship, Columbia, was reportedly almost off the assembly lines. Although the crowds were from the technologically sophisticated age of the 1970s, they exhibited the same awe and wonder over this craft—that might one day fly into space and back—as their early counterparts of the 1900s had when viewing the biplanes that were taking man up into the sky. While this was a day that made history for Stapleton, it was also a day of recapturing the historical excitement of early aviation.

## 1977 to 1979—Critical Years for Stapleton

During the last three years of the 1970s, discussion intensified over Stapleton's future. Numerous studies and strategies were debated, from leaving Stapleton alone to expanding onto Arsenal land or building an entirely new airport 40–50 miles from Denver. This intense debate was necessitated by continual growth of Stapleton's passenger and aircraft activities, brought on mainly by the federal government's deregulation of the airlines in 1977/1978.

In October 1978, Congress passed a partial deregulation bill that, in effect, gave an airline the right to add one new route a year and protect one route a year by vetoing another company's request for a new route. A. L. Feldman, president of Frontier Airlines, was quoted by the *Rocky Mountain News*, October 17, 1978, as saying of deregulation: "The public won the benefits of a freer marketplace. Increased competition, or the threat of it, should stimulate the airlines to provide better service and at the lowest possible price."

Deregulation also meant that the commercial carriers could drop any of their routes to smaller airports. Out of this evolved the "hub and spoke" concept, where the large commercial carriers began dropping their short-haul routes to small and medium-sized cities because they were unprofitable and began concentrating their operations in selected transfer points so they could shuffle their passengers from one of their own planes to another instead of to a competing airline's plane. From this came hub airports—there were 23 by the end of 1979—and within this group came four major "internal" airports—Chicago, Atlanta, Dallas–Ft. Worth and Denver—each serving a 1,000-mile radius. With this concentration of business by the large airlines came a resurgence of small, commuter airlines serving the cities dropped by the larger carriers, and these commuters had to fly into the hub airports in order to link up with the larger airlines.

What this meant for Stapleton in the late 1970s, was double digit growth in both aircraft operations and passenger statistics. In 1976, Stapleton had ranked sixth in total aircraft operations and seventh in passengers, with 13.7 million people passing through its facilities—by 1978, the airport ranked fourth in total operations and had 18.9 million passengers (a 23.8-percent increase over 1977). Also, by the beginning of 1979, there were 12 small to medium-sized airline companies flying into Denver from cities that had been dropped by the trunk line carriers. During these and previous years, Stapleton was the fastest growing airport in the country.

This growth spurred city, airport and airline officials into once again seriously debating whether or not Stapleton would have adequate facilities and runways in the future. Numerous studies were commissioned to evaluate the airport's needs by 2000 and to determine if it should be moved or not.

In August 1977, airport consultants presented a rough plan to city officials on airport expansion through 2000. Unlike the $165 million–$203 million cost projected by the consultants in 1976, this report called for $800 million worth of expansion. Robert Stapp, public relations director for Stapleton, was quoted by the *Rocky Mountain News*, August 17, as saying, "It would be almost inconceivable they would spend $800 million that was essentially for just a transitional facility."

Stapp, predicting Stapleton would be replaced by a new airport by 2000, would not release details of the report because they were considered only rough ideas. Part of the plan, however, was released, and it called for the existing 68 concourse gates to be increased to 100. When Stapp was asked if any new runways were in the proposal, he commented that no one could talk about new runways because of the Park Hill residents: "Those people over there have been crying for years about the present system. They'd raise hell if we talked about new runways."

A month later, in Washington, Transportation Secretary Brock Adams told Congress that certain major airports would need to be relocated. He said that "almost certainly" San Francisco, Boston, New York City and Philadelphia would need new airports, while Denver, Atlanta, Chicago, Minneapolis, St. Louis and Seattle "might" need new airports.

Stapleton's director, Michael, said that if a new airport was built, location choices would be limited, for the mountains blocked the west, and the Arsenal and residential areas blocked the north and south. The only direction to go was east—but such a move and such a facility would cost a staggering amount, he said, citing the $1 billion cost of the new Dallas–Ft. Worth airport.

Suggestions as to what to do with the airport were coming in from everywhere. One suggestion came from George Wallace, a member of the Arapahoe County Airport Authority. He recommended that instead of moving the airport, all that was needed was to move Stapleton's general aviation to Arapahoe Airport. By removing the three fixed-base general aviation operators—Combs-Gates, Beechcraft and Atlas Air Corporation—and all small planes from Stapleton, congestion would be relieved. Wallace pointed out that Arapahoe Airport, built in the late 1960s, was the eighteenth busiest in the United States, with 403,000 takeoffs and landings per year. It had three runways—one 8,500 feet long and two at 5,000 feet each—which he felt could handle the extra load from Stapleton. Also, Arapahoe Airport was centered on a 28,000-acre master zoning plan, which meant anyone who built on the land automatically gave up air rights over the land, thus avoiding situations similar to Stapleton's air rights problems with Rocky Mountain Arsenal.

Although the plan was sound, the three Stapleton fixed-base operators were reluctant to move—Combs-Gates had, in 1974, built an executive and business terminal costing $650,000, and Beechcraft had built a $1.5 million hangar in 1977. Further, Stapleton was reluctant to give up the revenues generated by general aviation.

By the end of 1977, it was reported that 15.3 million passengers had used the airport that year. Director Michael told the *Denver Post*, January 28, 1978, that the figure represented an 11 percent increase over 1976, which "points up Denver's growing importance as a commercial and recreational hub, but it poses serious problems. It means we will be in a constant state of construction. That means some inconvenience for the people who patronize the airport."

A month later Michael announced that Stapleton could handle a five-percent growth in commercial airline flights and a 10-percent growth in people for the next three or four years, but that would push the airport to its capacity. At that point, he said, the city would have to build more facilities and more runways—pointing out, however, that Stapleton had nowhere to grow for new runways.

On May 12, 1978, Mayor McNichols announced that Denver would commission a long-range study to select a site for a new airport, saying he would ask DRCOG to do it. He also expressed the hope that the state would pay for up to 75 percent of the new airport—estimating it would cost as much as $2 billion—because the facility would probably be located on state land and as much as 50 miles away from Denver. (At the time, state officials refused to comment until they could thoroughly study the issue.)

The next day, the *Rocky Mountain News* quoted Mayor McNichols as saying:

> As the only large-hub airport in a radius of 500 miles, Stapleton is a vital resource for the entire Rocky Mountain region. We are fully aware of our responsibility to the people of the region. We stand ready to work together with our neighbors to ensure a smooth transition towards a larger, more modern and more efficient regional airport.

McNichols also said he felt it would take 25–30 years to develop a new airport, so plans should be started immediately.

Fifteen days later, there was a news conference held at the airport, attended by representatives of various agencies and city and airport officials. Denver Councilman William Roberts said that "we have 12 to 15 years at maximum" to develop an airport, contradicting Mayor McNichols' 25–30 year projection. Roberts called for a new airport by 1990 and believed it was a waste to continue pouring money into an airport that would ultimately be moved. He advocated that revenues not be used on new construction but for retiring bonds and saving for when the airport did move.

Captain Tom Lindermann, area safety coordinator of the Air Line Pilots Association, was also at the news conference and was quoted by the *Denver Post*, May 28, 1978, as saying: "Stapleton Airport is at capacity today, not in the year 2000. We need to start planning for a new airport so we can be in it in 10 or 12 years."

Michael Harp, air traffic controller and PATCO representative, said at the conference that the runways were too narrow and too close to each other to be utilized completely in bad weather, which held up operations and created unsafe conditions. He also warned, "Only a handful of people know what is really going on in the air and on the runways here at Stapleton."

By August 1978, the DRCOG agreed to do the long-range study that McNichols had requested in May. DRCOG said the study would probably cost $550,000 to complete and that an outside consultant firm would be sought to do the technical work. The consultant firm that was chosen was Peat, Marwick, Mitchell & Co.

In October, Alan Merson, regional administrator of the Environmental Protection Agency (EPA), said in a speech to the Noise Control Institute at the University of Colorado that a possible solution to the Stapleton problem could be to build runways up to 20 miles from the metropolitan area and shuttle passengers back and forth from Stapleton in high-speed mass transit vehicles along the existing Union Pacific railroad tracks. He also said, as quoted by the *Rocky Mountain News*, October 15, 1978, "We have an airport that's grown up now right in the middle of a residential community." (This statement was historically inaccurate: residential areas grew up around the airport.)

Throughout the debates that raged over Stapleton, both Mayor McNichols and director Michael understood that a new airport would probably be necessary in the future. However, they also realized it was their job as city officials to ensure the existing airport remain a viable, safe and nationally ranked facility until a new airport was built and operational. To do this, construction and expansion had to continue, which it did: A $1.4 million, 38,000-square foot United cargo building was built in 1977; the main east-west runway was rebuilt in 1978; and two pedestrian bridges from the terminal to the third level parking lot were erected in 1978. As part of this concept of continual growth during these uncertain years, Mayor McNichols unveiled, on October 28, 1978, a "temporary" master plan.

Explaining why the plan was needed, Mayor McNichols reasoned that because it would take about three years for the DRCOG study to be completed and another 10 years to develop and build a new airport, a growth plan was needed to keep Stapleton abreast of increasing airport activity. The plan, done by Peat, Marwick, Mitchell & Co., called for the existing 68 concourse gates to be increased to 103 by 1990 and to 133 by 2000. Parking would also be increased from the present capacity of 6,000 cars to 7,600 by 1990 and 11,200 by 2000. No new runways were mentioned in the plan.

Councilman Roberts, at the unveiling, announced he would do everything in his power to block the plan, for he still believed there was no reason to spend money on Stapleton if it was to be moved in the future.

In April 1979, Mayor McNichols, speaking at a Denver Kiwanis Club meeting, said that every day that went by lessened the chances of building a new airport. He pointed out that the federal government was unlikely to pay for it and the overall costs could conceivably go as high as $1–$2 billion. And, he said, if the airport was moved Denver would play only a minor role in the new facility. Mayor McNichols felt the most likely occurrence, however, would be the expansion of Stapleton onto Arsenal land—a plan he had opposed in the 1960s when he had been manager of public works and deputy mayor. In the *Denver Post*, April 19, 1979, he stated that he had opposed the concept of building runways and a new terminal on the Arsenal because it had "looked to me like kind of an airplane roulette" but now felt this might be the only course of action left open to Stapleton.

One of the reasons for Mayor McNichols' negativism toward a new airport came from problems that were arising with the DRCOG site selection study. By spring of 1979, the study had still not gotten underway because the Denver City Council had delayed authorization for it. Because city funds would be used to partially finance the study, the agreement between Denver and DRCOG required manager of public works, Harold V. Cook, to concur with the findings. The city council felt that it, too, should have final approval of the study's findings. Mayor McNichols—as well as executives of DRCOG—opposed this idea, explaining that if the council got its way other governments represented on DRCOG might also want approval and the study would fall apart. The clash of wills between Mayor McNichols and the council—specifically Councilman Roberts who sponsored the idea—was finally resolved through a compromise whereby the council would be represented on DRCOG's Technical Advisory Committee.

By this time, the study's original timetable of 36 months was cut to 10 months as pressure for answers came from all sides. The estimated cost of $550,000 for the study also changed to $600,000, of which Stapleton would pay $200,000 and the FAA $400,000.

In September 1979, state officials came out in favor of expanding into the Arsenal because the cost of building a new airport was too high—some estimates were up to $6 billion. Governor Lamm said there was no way the state could fund such a project, which would be the biggest public works project in the state's history.

With the fear that Stapleton just might try and expand into Arsenal land, the Adams County Commissioners endorsed a Commerce City plan to annex land contiguous to the Arsenal. This endorsement was given, the commissioners said, in an effort to stop the possible expansion of Stapleton. Adams County officials made it known that they wanted to annex all land north of the Arsenal to box in land Stapleton might want for expansion.

In the summer of 1979, Peat, Marwick, Mitchell & Co. suggested three courses of action for the airport: build a new north-south runway east of the present two north-south runways and extend the western most north-south runway; build two north-south runways, one on each side of the existing ones and extend the 11,500-foot north-south; or decommission the two north-south runways and build three north-south runways at a slightly different angle than the present ones. All involved Arsenal land.

On November 7, 1979, in the midst of controversy over its future, Stapleton celebrated its fiftieth birthday—though the actual date was October 17. An aviation old-timers breakfast was held at the Timberline Restaurant, and afterwards, the Colorado Aviation Historical Museum—put together by the Colorado Aviation Historical Society—was dedicated on the mezzanine level of the terminal.

The airport had come a long way in 50 years. It had grown to more than 10 times its original 640-acre size, and it employed more than 10,000 people, a far cry from the 40 employees in 1929. The open-cockpit, canvas-winged biplanes that had sputtered down the four small gravel and dirt runways in 1929 had been replaced by jumbo jets, roaring along four concrete runways that ran miles in length. When the airport had had its opening ceremonies in 1929, there were three airline companies operating from its facilities—in 1979 there were 16 trunk line and regional carriers, and 10 commuter airlines. Although Stapleton had lost much, if not all, of its 1929 flavor, it still could boast of standing on the same ground it had first occupied 50 years before. Stapleton reflected the continuity of its own, as well as Denver's history.

By Stapleton's fiftieth anniversary, nothing definite had been decided concerning the airport's fate. The DRCOG site selection study would not be completed until 1980, and even with its completion the debates over what to do would go on.

The uncertainty of Stapleton's future in 1979 simply reflected a basic theme of uncertainty that had run through the airport's entire history. The 50-year growth of Stapleton had only been achieved through people—city, airport and airline officials and general citizens—who had put aside uncertainty and taken risks, beginning with Mayor Ben Stapleton who had taken a risk and bought 640 acres of sandy dunes far from downtown Denver. Although no one can accurately predict where Stapleton will be in the next 50 years, it can be said that Stapleton International Airport's future will be determined by those who continue to put aside uncertainties and take risks.

# Epilogue

On May 29, 1980, DRCOG unveiled its site options for a new airport (see map below). There were six choices: site one was directly north of Stapleton and west of Fort Lupton; site two was parallel to site one but east of Fort Lupton; site three included all of the Rocky Mountain Arsenal and more land to the north and east of the Arsenal; site four overlapped part of site three but was further southeast; site five was southeast of Stapleton near Barr Lake; and site six was north of Watkins and Bennett and east of Stapleton.

In the 1983 Denver mayorial election, both Dale Tooley and Federico Pena released a joint statement backing expansion onto Rocky Mountain Arsenal. In support of his pre-election promise, Mayor Pena has now firmly committed his administration to expanding the airport onto Arsenal land rather than moving it.

This does not mean, however, that the airport's future is secure — if nothing else, Stapleton has proved that its future is never predictable. Discussions and debates are still going on about the airport. It would be impossible to cover all the different points of view without beginning the history of Stapleton's next 50 years, a challenge we leave to a future volume.

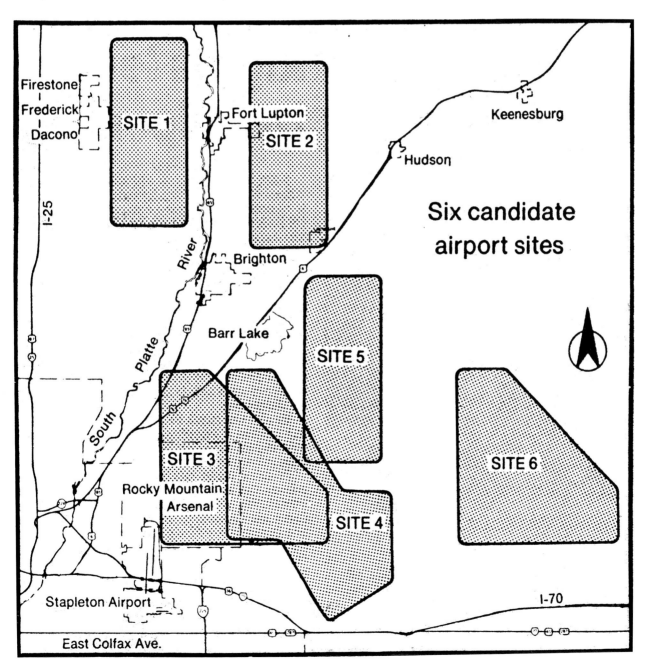

*One of Western's DC-3s, considered by many to be the best airplane ever built. Courtesy of Western Airlines.*

# Histories of the Airlines

Any history of Stapleton International Airport would not be complete without the histories of those airlines that have served Denver and its airport since the early years of commercial flight. The following pages give short histories of Western, United, Continental and Frontier airlines. As early aviation grew into a viable and working mode of transportation, these four airlines became important air carriers. They each have their own unique and fascinating story of those early years—how they sputtered, faultered, then rose off the ground to become the aviation giants of today.

## Western Airlines

Western Airlines, originally Western Air Express, holds the distinction of being the oldest continually operated air carrier in the United States, although United Airlines also claims that distinction (see a complete discussion of this claim under the history of United Airlines).

Western's incorporation papers were filed in Los Angeles on July 13, 1925. Harris M. (Pop) Hanshue, president and general manager, and Major Corliss C. Moseley, vice president of operations, were the driving force behind the infant airline. Hanshue came to Western Air Express after being a racecar driver and a distributor for the Apperson Jackrabbit car. He had limited aviation experience or knowledge, but he did believe in the future of aviation and was a good businessman. Moseley flew with the U.S. Army Air Corps in France during World War I. At the end of the war he joined the California National Guard before helping to form Western.

Both men saw the commercial possibilities of an airplane company after the Kelly Act was passed by Congress in February, 1925. This Act empowered the postmaster general to offer portions of the transcontinental airmail route to private contractors. The transcontinental route had been developed by the U.S. Post Office in 1919 and completed in 1920. The route traveled from New York City to Chicago, then on to San Francisco. "Feeder" routes had been established to link the main route (called the "Columbia" route) with population centers not on the route. After the Post

Office flew the mail for more than five years, Congress wanted to see if private enterprise could fly the routes more efficiently and safely. The Kelly Act made the feeder lines available for private contractor bidding in a plan to phase out the Post Office from all airmail service. The post office retained operation of the Columbia route until 1927, when it, too, was offered to private airlines.

On July 15, 1925, only two days after Western had filed its incorporation papers, the postmaster general advertised for bids on the feeder routes. With no operating capital and not a single plane or pilot, the new Western Air Express company bid on the Los Angeles–Salt Lake City route, via Las Vegas. (Salt Lake was one of the stops on the Columbia route.) With the transcontinental route going from New York to San Francisco, any airline company would have found the feeder route from Los Angeles to San Francisco more lucrative and easier to establish than a feeder route traversing barren, desert land. Western, however, chose to bid on the Los Angeles–Salt Lake City route. There was no official reason given for this decision, but unofficially it was reported that there was bad blood between the businessmen of Los Angeles and San Francisco over the decision to make San Francisco and not Los Angeles the western end of the transcontinental route. Western Air Express, it is postulated, did not want to give the businessmen of San Francisco the satisfaction of linking Los Angeles with the Columbia route via San Francisco and, therefore, took the more difficult 670-mile Salt Lake City route. On November 7, 1925, it was announced that Western had been awarded the route—now all the company needed was money, planes and pilots.

Finding pilots was no problem for Moseley, he went to his unit of the California National Guard. On December 1, 1925, Fred Kelly became the first pilot hired by Western. Later, Charles N. (Jimmy) James, Alva R. Degarmo and Maurice F. Graham were hired, all from Moseley's National Guard unit. These four men, the first four pilots of Western Air Express, became known as the "Four Horsemen."

Capital to initially fund the corporation, purchase the planes and establish the contracted route, was more difficult to obtain. Although airlanes had shown their military worth during World War I, they had yet to show their true commercial potential. Only the most farsighted businessmen in 1925 were willing to risk their capital on a fledgling airline company. Western did, however, find such men: People like Harry Chandler, publisher of the *Los Angeles Times,* and William M. Garland, real estate tycoon, saw the future of aviation and became a part of the original stockholders group.

For operating capital after the corporation was formed, Western approached the Ford Motor Company through a friend of Moseley's who was a Ford dealer in southern California. The Ford Company, at the time, was manufacturing a plane it had helped develop called the Ford-Stout. Because of an agreement between Western and Ford to buy seven of those planes, Western was able to raise $360,000, mostly from the Ford dealers in southern California. One of the stipulations Moseley had asked for in the agreement, however, was the right to reject the Ford-Stout after a representative of Western had reviewed the plane.

Moseley sent Fred Kelly—at the time the only pilot for Western—to Detroit where he tested the all-metal Ford-Stout. Kelly thought the plane would never be able to handle the tough, desert and mountain route, so he began looking for a new plane. While searching for a new aircraft, Kelly was introduced to the Douglas M-2 biplane (built by Donald Douglas), in Dayton, Ohio. Kelly was impressed with the plane's maneuverability and overall construction. He passed the word to Moseley that if Western wanted sturdy, reliable planes, they should buy the Douglas M-2s.

In Los Angeles, Moseley realized that when Western rejected the Ford-Stout plane it might mean the loss of some, if not all, of the $360,000 operating capital. He and Hanshue quickly raised another $100,000 as insurance against that possibility, then wired the Ford Motor Company that Western Air Express had rejected the Ford-Stout. When Ford did not pull its support from Western, Moseley went ahead and put in an order for six Douglas M-2 biplanes, costing $11,500 apiece.

The Douglas M-2 was a two-seater, open-cockpit biplane made of red fabric and wood. On the tail, Western placed its arrowhead logo—at first, there was only one plane with the distinctive Western logo (Moseley's plane), but quickly the entire fleet of M-2s carried the symbol.

The next step for Western was to find a field from which the company could fly. An old, vacant movie studio was found and converted into a hangar, and a landing field was laid out in front of it. The field became known as Vail Field and was located in the area that is now the City of Commerce, just outside of Los Angeles.

Western now had an airfield, planes, pilots and operating capital; it was time to establish the route from Los Angeles to Salt Lake City. In February 1926, the Four

Horsemen took off across the desert in a truck loaded with supplies and equipment to establish emergency landing strips. The men laid out canvas strips and landing markers (a canvas "V" signified the direction to land in, a canvas "T" meant landing in that area was at your own risk) along the route, and made arrangements with local farmers and ranchers to call in weather information to Western's headquarters. They also arranged with the Union Pacific Railroad to use the emergency telephone boxes placed along the railroad lines if they ever needed them. (At this point the railroads did not see the airplane as a threat to their freight and passenger business.)

Navigation in these early days of aviation was simply a matter of looking out of a plane and spotting landmarks that would be on a regular road map. The Four Horsemen decided the best way to navigate the Los Angeles–Salt Lake City route would be to follow the railroad lines (this was how most flyers found their way from place to place). It was also decided that each pilot would always fly on the right side of the train tracks to reduce the possibility of collision when visibility was poor.

After the route was properly marked, it was decided Kelly and Graham would be stationed in Los Angeles and DeGarmo and James in Salt Lake City. This way, there would be a constant flow of mail from city to city with two planes in the air at the same time.

With a total of 15 employees, six biplanes, a hangar and small airstrip, Western was ready to fly.

On April 17, 1926, the first flight of Western Air Express took off from Los Angeles bound for Salt Lake City, via Las Vegas, with another Western plane taking off from Salt Lake City bound for Los Angeles. By a toss of a coin between Kelly and Graham, Graham won the right to fly the historic flight out of Los Angeles. (James, in Salt Lake City, had won the right to fly to Los Angeles and flew out early the same morning.) Graham took off from Los Angeles at 7:45 A.M. with 256 pounds of mail. Clair Windsor, a famous movie actress, was on hand to help promote the event, and thousands of spectators cheered as Graham flew east.

Although airmail was the primary reason for Western's existence (for many years it would be the only true profit center for the airline), passengers were accepted. Any brave souls who wanted to try their luck with the birds, and "birdmen," were issued a parachute, goggles, leather cap and had to sit in an open cockpit with airmail bags at their feet. On May 23, 1926, Western took its first passenger aloft, Ben F. Redman, a Salt Lake City businessman. The one-way fare cost $90. About two weeks later, Maude Campbell bought a round trip ticket from Salt Lake City and became the first woman passenger Western carried. During her flight, she and the pilot passed notes back and forth about the weather, view and noise of the engine.

*The Douglas M-2 open cockpit biplane was the first plane flown by Western Air Express pilots. The company bought six of them in its first year of business, 1926, to fly the mail from Los Angeles to Salt Lake City. Courtesy of Western Airlines.*

From the start, flying mail was more lucrative than anyone had suspected. By the end of the first year of operation, Western had flown 328,892 air miles, carried 209 passengers and had a net profit of $1,029. The company continued to expand and grow successfully in 1927, and in October paid its shareholders their first dividend. On December 10, Western took over the airmail route between Cheyenne, Denver and Pueblo from Colorado Airways, and even further expansion was planned. At the end of this second year of operation, profits climbed to an incredible $306,974.

In June 1928, Western merged with Pacific Marine Airways, which operated between Los Angeles and Santa Catalina Island. Pacific Marine Airways billed itself as "the world's shortest overseas airline" and had first begun operating in 1922. Western also acquired interest in the Fokker Aircraft Corporation in 1928. This airplane manufacturer was the U.S. subsidiary of the Fokker Company in Germany. (When the government broke up the airlines in the 1930s, Fokker Aircraft Corporation became the North American Aviation manufacturing company).

Western's greatest challenge during these early years came in 1928, when the Guggenheim Fund for the Foundation of Aviation approached the airline and asked Western to develop a "model airway" between Los Angeles and San Francisco. The Guggenheim Foundation wanted to see if Western could prove that flying passengers, without mail, could be profitable. The foundation loaned Western $180,000 to develop the idea, with the only stipulation being that no airmail could be carried.

Hanshue and Mosely decided to accept the challenge. They realized, however, that their fleet of open-cockpit M-2, Boeing 95s and 90-B-4s (acquired in mergers or by purchase), were simply not the right planes for attracting or carrying the large number of passengers needed to make the route financially profitable.

To accommodate passengers, Moseley ordered three Fokker F-10 trimotor planes. These sealed cabin planes had been advertised as the "Leviathians of the air" and could hold 10–12 passengers. They required two pilots and had mahogany paneling, light pile carpeting and

In June 1928, Western Air Express merged with Pacific Marine Airways, which operated between Los Angeles and Santa Catalina Island. These were two of the passenger planes used for that service, a Sikorsky S-38 amphibian (1929), and a Boeing 204 Flying Boat (1928). Courtesy of Western Airlines.

wicker chairs as part of their passenger-oriented features. They also had a lavatory in the rear, and windows that could be opened in-flight for passengers who wanted a breath of fresh air.

Even with the comfort afforded by the F-10s, both Hanshue and Moseley believed they had to offer more to attract passengers. They arranged with the Pig 'n' Whistle, a Los Angeles restaurant, to make sandwiches which could be served on the flights. Another service was a free logbook called "The log of my flight between Los Angeles and San Francisco," so passengers could keep a detailed account of the flight. Western also hired a chauffeured Cadillac in Los Angeles and offered free limousine service exclusively to Western customers. This was the first recorded airport limousine service in the United States.

Nineteen hundred and twenty-eight was also a year of technological advances, which helped make air travel safer. On November 6, 1928, Western—in conjunction with Boeing Air Transport—became the first airline to use two-way radios in its planes. Although the range of the radios was limited, it was a start toward safer airplanes.

By the end of 1928, Western had gone from its original 15 employees and six airplanes to 143 employees and 25 aircraft. Expansion and diversification had been achieved through mergers with other airline companies and the acquisition of an airplane manufacturer. The total number of air miles flown by Western pilots and planes had jumped to 946,660.

In 1929, Western became one of the first three carriers to operate from Denver's new Municipal Airport. Western had been flying the mail into Denver since December 10, 1927, and landing at Humphrey's Field (for years Denver's official airmail field), until construction of the ultramodern Denver Municipal Airport in 1929. For years, Western was the only major air carrier serving Denver and helped the fledgling airport by supplying it with a steady flow of revenue. But in 1934, when the government cancelled all airmail contracts across the country, Western lost the authority to fly into Denver and it was only in 1944, with the purchase of Inland Airlines, that Western resumed flying into the Mile High City.

Throughout 1929, Western continued to grow and prosper—with the exception of the Guggenheim experiment. After a year of operating the Los Angeles–San Francisco run without carrying mail, it was determined that carrying only passengers was a financial failure. It was, however, an incredible success with the passengers, and Western began a concerted effort to attract passengers on all its flights—although the flying of mail would remain its largest source of revenue for years.

As Western Air Express entered the 1930s, the Great Depression was taking hold. As many peoples' fortunes fluctuated through this unstable period, so did Western's. At one point, through a series of mergers, Western became the largest airline in the world, with 15,832 miles of routes. But by the mid- to late 1930s, the company had shrunk to almost the same size it had been in 1926.

In 1930, however, with its new status as the largest airline in the world, Western ordered two of the new Fokker F-32s to accommodate its increasing number of passengers. The F-32 was a four-engine plane that could seat 32 people in a comfort and style never before rivaled. The seats were covered in alligator skin and stuffed with rubber balls for added comfort. The plane was divided into eight compartments and had steward call buttons, a smoking compartment and walnut paneling throughout. Painted red with gold and black edges and wings of silver, these incredible aircraft cost an unheard of $110,000 each.

But the new F-32s were not without their problems. The engines were mounted tandem, two engines back-to-back on each side of the plane. The back engines, it was found, did not receive enough air during flight and, therefore, were constantly overheating. Because of this problem and the high cost of maintaining the planes, the F-32s were phased out of Western service after only two years (one of the two was scrapped and other was converted into a gas station in downtown Los Angeles).

During 1930, the federal government once again stepped into the aviation picture, affecting Western's future. In an effort to consolidate the aviation industry, the postmaster general put pressure on Western and Transcontinental Air Transport to merge. Hanshue, as president of Western, fought the merger, fearing Western would lose its identity in such a move. Although the merger did go through, Hanshue was able to retain independent status for Western Air Express by merging the majority of the company but keeping Western's corporate identity. Most of Western's lucrative routes were part of the merger so that Western Air Express was left with only its original Los Angeles–Salt Lake City route, a Los Angeles–San Diego route and the Pueblo–Denver–Cheyenne run.

After the merger was complete, Hanshue became president of the new company, Transcontinental and Western Air, Inc. (TWA), and left some trusted personnel to run the now greatly reduced Western Air Express. Because of illness, Hanshue had to resign his new post after only eight months and after he recovered he returned to Western.

During this time of merger, 1930-1934, advances were being made in air safety. One of the biggest factors in air safety was the weather. Western had established weather stations along its routes, but the company's forecasting ability was rated as a mediocre 65 percent. In 1932, Jimmy James, one of the Four Horsemen and then vice president of operations, interviewed a young

*The Boeing 247D was one of Western's early passenger planes. Courtesy of Western Airlines.*

*In 1930 Western ordered two Fokker F-32s as passenger planes. These planes could seat 32 in a style never rivaled. They had alligator skin seats stuffed with rubber balls, reclining seats, two lavatories, two galleys, a smoking compartment and walnut paneling throughout. They cost $110,000 a piece. Courtesy of Western Airlines.*

student from California Tech, Irving Krick. Krick believed he could accurately forecast the weather through a Norwegian method of studying air masses. James was skeptical, hiring Krick as only a mail clerk, but told him to forecast in his spare time.

Shortly after being hired, Kirck predicted one of Western's planes would be flying directly into a storm if it was not grounded immediately. Krick convinced James to ground the plane and later it was learned that everything Krick had forecast was true. As a result of that incident, Krick was promoted to Western's meteorologist and brought the company's forecasting record up to an incredible 96.1 percent accuracy. The Western public relations office began an advertising campaign around Krick's forecasting, stating that "Western Air Express planes always have tailwinds." (Later, Krick left Western to teach, and during World War II he was responsible for the weather forecasting that dictated the day of the D-Day invasion.)

In 1934, all airmail contracts were cancelled when corruption was discovered in the system of awarding the contracts. For a short time, the Army flew the mail, but after numerous aerial accidents, Congress passed the Air Mail Bill of 1934, which returned the mail to private enterprise. There were, however, certain stipulations to the bill. One of these was that no airline chief who had been in power during the old contracts could continue serving the same company. Because of this, Hanshue resigned from Western in 1934 and became president of Eastern Airlines for a short time until his death in 1935.

With the airmail controversy also came antitrust action by the government against the airline companies. During the late 1920s and early 1930s, airline companies had been merging and forming larger companies while also diversifying into the aircraft manufacturing industry. When the government stepped in, one of its actions forced the separation of Western and Transcontinental. The company that had been formed in 1930, Transcontinental Western Airlines, went on to become Trans World Airlines (TWA), while Western was left with almost what it had started with nearly nine years before: the Los Angeles–Salt Lake City route and a route from Los Angeles to San Diego.

Although Western was hurt financially by the separation, it was determined to stay alive. In 1935, to attract passengers, Western decided to employ stewardesses on its flights. Stewards had been used on the Guggenheim experiment, but it was not until 1935 that Western began using stewardesses. The company advertised for the new jobs, expecting only 10–20 applicants: 200 women applied. Only two were hired at first—Ursula Brown was the first, and she served on a Boeing 247-D.

Also during this time, Western purchased National Parks Airways, which had the route from Salt Lake City to Great Falls, Montana. This route would later become important as Great Falls became the stepping stone for Western's expansion into Canada during early 1941.

In 1939, Western and United Airlines almost merged. The two companies had been cooperating with each other for years along similar routes. Although the current president of Western fought the merger, it was approved by the two companies and the application was sent to the Civil Aeronautics Board for its approval. Approval was denied, however, and Western continued on its own.

In 1941, Western Air Express officially dropped the "Express" from its name. Many felt that that word connoted cargo while the company was then trying to emphasize passenger services. In actuality, the word express had originally stood for speed, not cargo.

Also in 1941, immediately following the Japanese attack on Pearl Harbor, the government requisitioned many planes from the airline companies. Western was left with only three DC-3s and one Lockheed Lodestar but was given the job of training pilots for the military and flying material up to Alaska. The company established training schools in Salt Lake City and in California and began flying to Alaska under the government's operation "Sourdough." Facing some of the coldest winters in Alaska's history, with temperatures of 65–70 degrees below zero, Western planes and pilots worked almost around the clock. By the end of the war, Western had flown 67 million air miles and carried 22 million pounds of cargo for the war effort.

The readjustment to civilian life was tough for many airlines. Financially, Western was in trouble, supporting 2,600 employees and being overextended on routes. At one time the company had to sell some of its airplane tires to make the payroll. But Terrell C. Drinkwater, a Colorado attorney who had become president in January 1947, was determined to keep the company alive. He began a campaign called "constructive contraction," whereby the airline would concentrate on already established routes and develop them to their full potential before expanding further. Reaching the routes' full potential involved the development of on-board services to attract more people, and backing those services up with advertising campaigns.

By far the most famous service Western began offering during this time was the champagne flight. Known first as "The Californian," these flights later became known as "Champagne Flights." On board steak dinners and champagne were served, and men received cigars and women perfume and orchids. The advertising campaign that followed this service was developed in 1955 and began appearing on television in 1956. The advertising centered around the Very Important Bird ("V.I.B.") who lounged on a pillow propped up on the tail section of a Western plane. This

V.I.B. would state: "Western Airlines—the *only* way to fly." The bird worked so well it was used for 14 years before the company decided to retire it for fear of overexposure. But it was brought out of retirement four years later because of its popularity.

Also in the 1950s, Western inaugurated flights to Mexico City, aided in the Korean airlift and celebrated its silver anniversary.

In 1960, Western Airlines entered the jet age by leasing two Boeing 707s. Also during that year, the government dealt Western a setback of sorts when it decided to delay international route awards in the Pacific, specifically a long-awaited route to Hawaii that CAB had recently awarded to Western. Western had first requested a route to Hawaii in 1944 to compete with Pan American, but the government had decided to postpone awarding the route until World War II was over. Western was finally granted the route on July 4, 1969.

On July 1, 1967, an important merger took place between Western and Pacific Northern airlines. This merger opened up routes for Western into Alaska, adding 3,388 miles of routes to nine Alaskan cities. With the merger, Western then covered 14,156 route miles to 44 cities in 12 western states, Alaska, Canada and Mexico.

Through the 1970s, Western continued to grow and expand. By 1979, the airline served 44 cities in 16 states and the District of Columbia, and Canada and Mexico. Western had grown in more than 50 years from six Douglas M-2 open-cockpit biplanes and 15 employees to 76 modern aircraft and more than 11,000 employees.

## United Airlines

In July 1931, with the filing of its incorporation papers, United Airlines was born as a management corporation for four individual airline companies: Varney Air Lines, begun April 6, 1926; Pacific Air Transport, begun September 15, 1926; Boeing Air Transport, begun July 1, 1927; and National Air Transport, begun September 1, 1927. Philip G. Johnson, president of Boeing Manufacturing and Air Transportation Company, became United's chief executive, guiding and establishing policies for the four airlines.

*United Airlines was born as a management corporation in 1931 for four individual airlines: Varney Air Lines, Pacific Air Transport, National Air Transport, and Boeing Air Transport. This Ford Tri-Motor was one of the early planes United used to carry passengers. Courtesy of United Airlines.*

(Because of Varney Air Line's first official flight on April 26, 1926, from Pasco, Washington, to Eldo, Nevada, United has claimed to be the oldest air carrier in the United States. This claim is disputed by Western Airlines, which believes United's use of Varney's operating date is like a son using his father's birthday as his own. Western believes it is the oldest continually operated air carrier in the nation, citing its date of incorporation, July 13, 1925. Even if a merged company's founding date is used—as United has done with Varney—Western still maintains it deserves the title of oldest air carrier, for in June 1928, Western purchased Pacific Marine Airways, which had been operating from Los Angeles to Catalina Island since 1922—four years before Varney began flying.)

With the consolidation of the four airlines in 1931, United held substantial interests in the growing air transportation industry. Boeing Air Transport (BAT) and National Air Transport (NAT) flew the complete U.S. airways number one, or transcontinental route, of New York City–Chicago–San Francisco. Also, Boeing Air Transport was composed of the Boeing Airplane Company and Pratt & Whitney, an engine manufacturer.

It was not unusual in the early 1930s for an air carrier to hold major interest in airplane manufacturing companies. But the forming of such diversified airlines brought about government scrutiny over possible violation of antiturst laws. This scrutiny played an indirect role in the uncovering of corruption in the awarding of airmail contracts during the early 1930s. As a result, in 1934, the government cancelled all airmail contracts and the Army began flying the mail.

Within a few months, however, the Army had numerous aerial accidents and the government returned the airmail to the private sector through the Air Mail Act of 1934. Certain provisions, though, were part of the legislation. These provisions stated no airline that had held old contracts could bid on the new ones, and all airline company chiefs who had been in power during the old contracts had to resign. To circumvent these provisions, many airlines simply reorganized under a new name.

In 1934, United reorganized, changing from a management company to a full-fledged operating corporation. Johnson became president of United Aircraft and Transportation Corporation (the holding company for three separate companies: United Air Lines Transportation Company, Boeing Airplane Company and United Aircraft Corporation), and William (Pat) Patterson, formerly vice president of United Airlines became president of United Airlines.

Patterson, one of the major forces in the history of United Airlines, had worked for Wells Fargo Bank and had authorized a $5,000 loan to Pacific Air Transportation (PAT) in 1926. He then became financial advisor for PAT and assisted in the merger with BAT in 1928. This landed him the job of assistant to the president of Boeing before the merger that formed United. Patterson moved from president of United to chairman of the board in 1963 and retired in 1966, but during his nearly 30 years as president of United he directed, shaped and guided the company through the infancy of flight into the jet age. In 1934, Patterson developed the "Rule of Three" that would guide United for decades: "Safety, Passenger Comfort and Dependability."

During its early years, United learned a tough lesson in obsolescence. In 1932, while still in its management stage, United ordered 59 new Boeing 247s, which carried 10 passengers and traveled at 180 miles per hour. For a single year United was able to claim it had the fastest, most modern service available. By 1934, the last of the B-247s had arrived, but the competition had already surpassed United—in 1934 and 1935 two major competitors began using the DC-2s and DC-3s, which were faster, quieter and could hold more people than the B-247. Instantly, it seemed to United, it had the slowest, smallest and noisiest planes in the skies.

In 1935, United first flew into Denver Municipal Airport. On a lease agreement with Wyoming Air Service, which had been flying the Denver-Cheyenne route, United began flying Wyoming's B-247s into Denver from Cheyenne. On December 23, 1936, at the insistence of Denver businessmen and citizens, United applied to the Post Office to have Denver designated as a regular airmail stop on the transcontinental route. Before this time, the Denver-Cheyenne route had merely been a spur line off the main route. On May 11, 1937, the application was approved, and four days later, a United DC-3 took off from Denver heading for New York City, linking Denver by a one-company, coast-to-coast service for the first time. This was the beginning of twice daily flights to the East.

United's flights in and out of the Mile High City were, however, only during the day, for Denver Municipal did not have the proper facilities for scheduled night flying. The government had prepared a plan for aiding airports in the building of night-flying facilities but because Denver was not officially a part of the transcontinental route, it was low on the government's priorities list, with a waiting list of almost two years. United decided to take the initiative, and with the assurance that the government would later buy the facilities, United constructed intermediate fields between Denver and Grand Island, Nebraska, at Akron, Colorado, and Hays Center, Nebraska, installing radio range stations. These facilities were finished in 1938, and in 1939 the government purchased them from United.

While United was developing the Denver transportation market, it was also developing its whole operation, trying new ways of attracting passengers. Patterson decided that the cold sandwiches served aboard United flights were not a good enough selling point, and in

1936 he hired a Swiss chef to open a flight kitchen in Oakland, California. This was the first flight kitchen established by an airline. By 1979, United had 19 flights kitchens in 17 cities, spending millions of dollars a year to prepare meals for its passengers.

At the outbreak of World War II, United formed the Victory Corporation to counteract possible government takeover. This corporation contracted with the government to provide air carrier service for the cost of operation plus one dollar. United trained military pilots and flew cargo for the government throughout the war.

In 1940, United began constructing a maintenance operation center in San Francisco, but because of the war this facility was not completed until April 1948. United also expanded its training facilities during the war. United had always placed strong emphasis on the training of its pilots. The Boeing School of Aeronautics (part of BAT) had been formed in Oakland in 1929 and became a division of United Airlines in the 1934 reorganization. This training center was enlarged, under government contract, during the war and was moved to Cheyenne in 1942. In 1943, it was moved to Denver, where it later developed into the largest training school for pilots and crews in the nation.

In August 1968, United's training school moved into a new $30 million, 289,000-square-foot facility located in Denver. By 1979, a staff of more than 500, utilizing the most advanced technological equipment, trained up to 160 pilots a day from United, the FAA, and Air Force as well as European, South American and Pacific area airlines, and from private and business aviation companies. (United pilots are required to return to the flight school every six months for refresher courses.) In training the pilots, the school utilized 13 airplane simulators and 10 cockpit procedure trainers, giving students a good simulation of takeoffs, landings and in-flight activities. The most modern simulators were of the DC-10 and B-747, which had a complete hydraulic system that realistically exhibited a sense of forward/backward, left/right and up/down motion. Each simulator was a sealed duplicate of a cockpit, and a film of whatever simulation was desired was shown on screens that replaced the cockpit's windows.

*In 1943 United's training school was moved from Cheyenne, Wyoming to Denver. In August 1968 the school was moved into a new $30 million facility — just west of Stapleton's terminal — which houses the most advanced technological equipment for training. Up to 160 pilots a day from all different airlines are trained there.*

After World War II, United arranged with Western Airlines to take over the Denver–Los Angeles route. On September 1947, CAB approved the transfer and United began five daily round trips. Following this new route, it was announced that United would move its base of operations to Denver's airport. After studying 40 possible locations, Denver was chosen for its geographically central location on United's route system. More than 300 United employees moved to the new operations base in 1948. In 1953, United's Denver office moved into a new building that had been built for the airline through an airport bond issue.

During the 1950s, United continued to strive for better service to its passengers. In April 1953, United inaugurated for-men-only "Executive" flights between Chicago and New York City. This service, while some might have found it chauvinistic, was nonetheless highly successful and continued for 17 years until January 1970. This special flight was only one of the many promotions and advertising campaigns developed by United through its history. By far the most famous advertising campaign was "Fly the Friendly Skies of United," begun in October 1965. Another promotion, "Take Me Along," begun in September 1967, was designed to sell two seats at a time instead of one. These campaigns, and many more, made United a consistent leader in national advertising and promotion.

While trying to attract passengers, United was also trying to expand its operations. In June 1961, United completed the largest merger in its history with Capital Airlines—a carrier that had begun carrying mail between Pittsburgh and Cleveland in 1927. The merger added 7,000 employees to United as well as 7,250 new route miles. Overnight, United was transformed into the largest airline in the Free World—a distinction United retained through 1979.

The 1960s was an important decade for United, not only because of its merger with Capital, but because in 1969 United went through another reorganization. This change created UAL, Inc. and made United Airlines a wholly owned subsidiary of the corporation. In 1970, Western International Hotels became a second subsidiary of UAL, Inc.; in 1975 GAB Business Services (the nation's oldest and largest independent insurance adjustment corporation) became a third subsidiary; and in 1979 Mauna Kea Properties became the fourth.

By 1970, however, United found itself in financial trouble, with losses of close to $40 million by the end of the year. This was due in part to a recession in the travel market and to CAB's decision to open the Hawaii routes to other airlines—where United had had a virtual monopoly. Because of United's financial situation, UAL's board of directors decided a change in management was needed, and made Edward Carlson (chairman and chief executive officer of Western International Hotels), president and chief executive officer of United.

"Eddie" Carlson jumped right into the job, determined to bring United out of the red. During the first year, Carlson logged 187,000 miles, talking with employees and trying to determine how to reorganize United so it would function profitably. Taking drastic measures to correct a drastic situation, Carlson cut flight schedules, furloughed several thousand employees, cancelled airplane orders and restructured United into three divisions: Eastern, Central and Western. These divisions were to operate in competition with each other and be responsible for operating in the black.

By 1974, Carlson's plan had worked; United showed a $86 million profit at the end of the year and was able to pay its shareholders dividends for the first time in more than three years. To match this upswing in the company—and as part of the upcoming American Bicentennial—United introduced a new logo (which it still retains), changed its official name from United Air Lines to United Airlines and modified Patterson's rule of three to read: "Safety, Service, Profitability, Integrity and Responsibility."

By 1979, the company served 113 cities in 32 states and Canada, on a 19,255 route-mile system; maintained 19 flight kitchens in 17 cities; and employed more than 45,000 people. It also boasted the most advanced and modern reservations and passenger information system, the Apollo. With its executive offices northwest of O'Hare Airport, its maintenance facilities in San Francisco, and its operation base, flight training school and a computer center in Denver, United retained the title of largest airline in the Free World.

### Some Firsts United Calls Its Own:

| | |
|---|---|
| December 1940 | first to operate all-cargo flights |
| 1957 | first transcontinental airline to equip its fleet with radar |
| 1963 | first to use dry ice seeding at airports to dispel supercooled fog |
| August 1967 | first to fly a billion passenger miles in a single month |
| 1973 | first to implement a computerized freight monitoring system |
| 1974 | first to automate ticket printing by teletype for commercial accounts |
| 1977 | first to come out in favor of government deregulation of U.S. airlines |
| 1977 | first to establish a guaranteed air fare |
| 1978 | first to order the Boeing 767 aircraft |

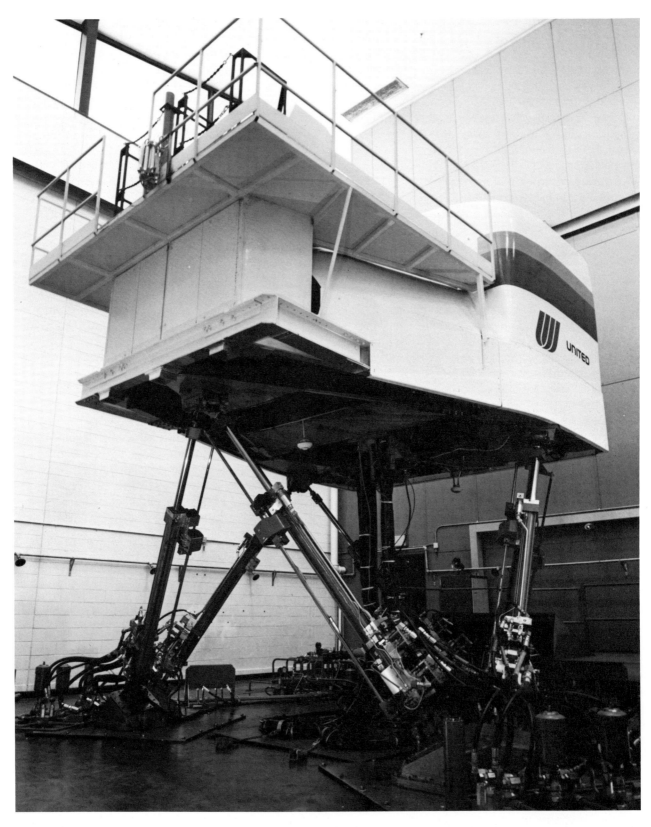

*Electronic educator. Training of United pilots who fly the Boeing 747 includes sessions in the 747 simulator, which electronically duplicates the flight characteristics of the jumbo jet. The simulator has a six-degree motion system and other features to enhance its realistic performance. The simulator costs more than $3.5 million. Courtesy of United Airlines.*

*There are 13 simulators at the United training center. United has at least one simulator for every type of aircraft it flies. Pilot trainees for many foreign and other U.S. airlines receive training at United's facility on a contract basis.*

## Continental Airlines

More than most airlines, Continental's history is the story of one man: Robert F. Six. Although many airlines had their pioneers—United's Willian Patterson, Western's Harris Hanshue, American's C. R. Smith, Eastern's Eddie Rickenbacker—Continental had the leadership of Six for more than 40 years, during which time aviation changed from open-cockpit biplanes to supersonic jets. For one man to remain a moving force in an industry that had metamorphosized countless times, it is a tribute to that man's scope of understanding and tenacity.

Robert Six learned to fly in a single engine OX-5 Alexander Eagle Rock biplane and, in 1929, at the age of 22 received his pilot's license. During that time, Six bought a plane and formed Valley Flying Service, which sold scenic rides. Deciding he wanted a full transport rating, Six enrolled in the first flying class given by Boeing Air Transport, which later became a part of United Airlines. Unfortunately, Six was expelled after training officials discovered he was recruiting class members to help him work on a hot rod plane he was flying on weekends.

During the depression, Six's Valley Flying Service folded, but in 1936, Six met Tommy Fortune Ryan III, who told him about an opportunity to buy into the Southwest Division of Varney Speed Lines (different from United's Varny Airlines). Varney had just won the airmail contract for El Paso, Texas, to Pueblo, Colorado, and needed money to operate the route. Six was introduced to Louis Mueller, who, with Walter T. Varney, had formed Varney Speed Lines in 1934. Deciding Varney was a good investment, Six bought into the company for $90,000 (taking out a loan with his father-in-law) and on July 15, 1936, became general manager.

To operate the airmail route Varney needed airplanes, so Six and Mueller went to Lockheed and bought three twin-engine Lodestars. Each plane cost $39,500 but Six talked Lockheed into a mere $5,000 down for each, with the loan for the rest of the money secured by Six and Muellers' homes and other personal property.

Knowing that to be successful Varney had to fly into Denver, Six and Mueller made a deal in 1937 with Pat Patterson of United to buy the routes of Wyoming Air Service for $50,000. United took the Denver-Cheyenne route and Varney took the Pueblo-Denver route. In October 1937, Six moved all of Varney's 16 employees to Denver from El Paso, making Denver the company's new headquarters. Later that year, the corporate name was changed to Continental Air Lines, Inc., and on February 3, 1938, Six was named president.

During World War II, Six served in the Army Air Transport Command as a lieutenant colonel and later as a reserve officer in charge of Continental's bomber modification center in Denver. In 1944, Continental won a series of routes from CAB so that the company service, then, included Texas, New Mexico, Oklahoma and Kansas.

In the 1950s, Continental continued to grow, with a variety of routes and an interchange service with other airlines: In 1951, an interchange service with American Airlines to the West Coast began with a route extension from San Antonio to Houston; in 1952, a service began with Mid Continent Air Lines between Denver and St. Louis via Kansas City; in 1953, service was started with United between Tulsa, Wichita and Seattle via Denver; and in 1955 absorption of Pioneer Airlines' routes gave Continental service to Dallas/Fort Worth and other Texas and New Mexico cities.

Continental service between Chicago and Los Angeles via Denver and Kansas City began in 1957, making Continental a major trunk line carrier. This new route boosted Continental's system so that by 1958 it covered eight states and 52 municipalities between Chicago and the Gulf of Mexico, the Mississippi River and the West Coast.

In July 1963, Six decided to move Continental's headquarters from Denver to Los Angeles. After being in Denver for more than 25 years, Continental's move, as officially stated by Six, came about because Los Angeles was the economic and geographical focal point of the airline. Unofficially, many felt Continental's move came in part from Denver's push to increase commercial airlines' landing fees at Stapleton to pay for expansion costs. Other unofficial reasons included Denver's refusal to give Continental a tax break, and the reluctance of Six's third wife, actress Audrey Meadows, to make Denver her home.

By 1964, Continental had obtained international status by providing contract flights for the Military Airlift Command (MAC) to South Vietnam, Thailand, Okinawa, the Philippines, Honolulu, Japan, South Korea, Guam and Taiwan. This was followed, in 1968, by a Department of Interior contract to provide service to the Trust Territory of the Pacific Islands, better known as Micronesia. The service—flown by a Continental subsidiary, Air Micronesia—included the islands of Majuro, Kwajalein, Ponape, Truk, Yap, Palau, Rota and Saipan, as well as Hawaii, Johnston Island, Guam and Okinawa.

In early 1969, Continental was ranked eighth among the nation's 11 trunk line carriers and was still growing. In June 1969, the airline grew by nearly 10 percent with CAB's approval to connect Denver with Portland, Seattle, San Antonio, Houston and New Orleans.

Another big step for Continental came in February 1974, when the airline began flying from Houston to

Miami. This route, gained after long legal proceedings, finally gave Continental true transcontinental status. A year later, at Six's recommendation, Continental's board of directors named Alexander Damm president and chief operating officer of Continental, and Six was elected chief executive officer and chairman of the board, retaining these titles through 1979 (Six officially retired April 1, 1982 after more than 45 years with Continental).

By 1979 Continental, using the "Proud Bird," an advertising campaign started in 1965, was serving 53 cities through 13 states and the South Pacific; a far cry from that 520-mile route first flown in 1934 between El Paso and Pueblo.

*In 1937 Continental Airlines was born from Varney Speed Lines. Robert F. Six, the moving force behind Continental for more than 45 years, had moved Varney Speed Lines headquarters up to Denver from El Paso in October of 1937, then later that year changed the company's name to Continental. Courtesy of the Western History Department, Denver Public Library.*

*One of Contintental's early passenger planes, a Lockheed Lodstar. Courtesy of the Western History Department, Denver Public Library.*

*In July 1963 Six decided to move Continental's headquarters from Denver to Los Angeles. Officially, the reason was given that Los Angeles was in a more centrally located position for Continental than Denver. Unofficially, many thought the move came because of arguments that had occurred between Denver city officials and airline executives over landing fees. Courtesy of the Western History Department, Denver Public Library.*

## Frontier Airlines

Frontier Airlines was officially born June 1, 1950, with the merging of three small feeder airlines: Monarch, Challenger and Arizona. By 1979, Frontier had grown into one of the largest regional air carriers in the United States and was the only major airline with its headquarters in Denver.

Monarch Airlines, the first of Frontier's predecessors to become operational, was founded by Ray M. Wilson and F. W. Bonfils (of the *Denver Post* family) in 1946. The purpose of the company was to serve small Rocky Mountain towns and communities that were being dropped by the trunk line carriers after World War II.

Trunk service was being discontinued to small towns all across the United States as the large airlines began utilizing four-engine planes and concentrating on major routes. To take their place, feeder, or "puddle-jumper," airlines like Monarch came into being.

On November 27, 1946, Monarch's inaugural flight from Denver to Durango—with stops in Colorado Springs, Pueblo, Canon City and Monte Vista—took off from Stapleton Airfield carrying a load of airmail, cargo and a lone G.I. Although the plane did not arrive in Durango that day—the airfields were too muddy from a recent storm—Monarch's initial staff of 150 was confident of the airline's future.

The new airline had been able to obtain three routes from the CAB in 1946. Along with the Denver-Durango route, Monarch also flew from Denver to Grand

Junction and from Albuquerque to Salt Lake City. Because most of the routes through the Rockies were not established Federal Airways and, therefore, did not have beacons or radio beams for navigation, Monarch placed its own navigational "H" markers along its routes to assure day, night and all weather flying. Ray Wilson—one of Colorado's aviation pioneers whose pilot's license was signed by Orville Wright and who had been operating a flying school in Park Hill before forming Monarch—explained one of the unique difficulties Monarch had with the H markers:

> In 1946 we were flying people through the mountains using what were called H markers. There would be one at the starting point and one at the destination, both of which transmitted a signal. Lining up the signals, one in front and one in back of the plane, the pilot knew he was flying in a straight line. On longer flights there would be a series of H markers spread out along the way.
>
> Well, one day one of our good pilots was flying in the afternoon when he ran into some clouds. Just then his forward radio signal went out, so he turned around and flew back to Durango. He called in to the Denver office and said, "Well, I guess I'll have to stay here because the radio signal in front of me went out." We got on the phone to the man near the H marker and asked him what was up. Well, he explained that the generator running the H marker had a limited capacity and milking time was right around 5 o'clock, so, he had turned everything off to milk the cows.

A year after Monarch was formed, Challenger Airlines began operations. On May 5, 1947, Challenger started flying from Salt Lake City to Denver via five Wyoming communities in the southern part of the state. In the summer, the airline added two more routes, one between Billings and Salt Lake City via the Big Horn Basin, and the other between Riverton, Wyoming and Denver. The airline's headquarters was originally Salt Lake City, but after a few months of operations it was moved to Denver. Challenger and its DC-3s called "Sunliners," proved their worth during a mammoth blizzard that struck most of Wyoming in February 1949. Challenger flew tons of foodstuffs to a population that had been immobilized by roof-high snowdrifts.

The third airline that became a part of Frontier was Arizona Airways. Begun in 1946, Arizona flew intrastate routes radiating from Pheonix for nearly two years before the CAB certified it. Operating without a federal certificate meant no federal subsidiaries, so to make ends meet, Arizona flew scenic flights from Phoenix to the Grand Canyon on weekends. Unfortunately, by the time the CAB certified the company in the summer of

1948, Arizona did not have the funds to begin scheduled interstate flights along the CAB approved routes.

While Arizona was struggling to survive, Monarch and Challenger decided, in December 1949, to merge their general office and maintenance operations in a move to economize and cut costs. In the spring of 1950, CAB approved the further merger of Challenger and Monarch with Arizona's routes—out of this merger came Frontier Airlines. Monarch was the only corporate entity to survive the merger, and Monarch's president, Hal S. Darr, became Frontier's president, and Ray Wilson became vice president of operations.

The new Frontier Airlines started with 400 employees and 12 DC-3s. It served 40 cities in seven states in the Rocky Mountain West and the Southwest. To drum up business in its early years, Frontier staged air fairs in many of the small towns and cities it served. The airline would offer 20-minute flights for three dollars and occasionally drop balloons and timetables—some good for free flights—over the town.

Two years after its forming, Frontier received CAB approval to serve 25 more cities east and west across Nebraska and between Denver, Omaha and Kansas City, and on a north-south route between Denver and Minot via intermediate communities in western Nebraska, South Dakota and North Dakota. These new routes became operational in late 1958 and early 1959.

By 1960 Frontier was carrying 30,000 passengers a month through 10 states and had 1,081 employees, mostly working out of the new general office building at Stapleton. During the next five years Frontier continued to expand its routes and, in 1966, was the first regional carrier to introduce the Boeing 727 tri-jets into service. While entering the jet age, Frontier was, for a short while, the most active airline at Stapleton, with 133 landings and 133 takeoffs a day.

In October 1967, Frontier merged with Central Airlines, which had begun operations from Fort Worth in 1949. The merger boosted Frontier's air service to 114 cities in 14 states. Within a year, Frontier also became a totally jet-propelled airline with the retirement of its last DC-3.

Although the early 1970s were financially difficult for Frontier because of aircraft costs and a slowdown in passenger travel, by the mid-1970s the airline was gaining ground again. In July 1974, Frontier became an international airline with inauguration of service to Winnipeg in Manitoba, Canada. Four years later, on November 3, 1978, Frontier added another country to its operations with the start of service to Mazatlan and Guadalajara, Mexico.

By 1979, Frontier had gained a strong financial footing, reporting a profit of $21.7 million, and was serving more than 70 points in 26 states, Canada and Mexico—no one could ever again call Frontier a puddle-jumper airline.

Thirty years ago uniforms worn by airline stewardesses accented the "nurse" look — mainly because early stewardesses had to be registered nurses. Shown in the photo at top are stewardesses of Challenger Airlines. In marked contrast are the uniforms worn by today's stewards and stewardesses, now called flight attendants. Shown below are uniforms introduced in 1977 by Frontier, styled to accent "professionalism and versatility."

Frontier Airlines was formed when three small "feeder" airlines merged: Monarch, Challenger and Arizona. Monarch flew to small Rocky Mountain towns not serviced by other airlines. It was founded by Ray Wilson and F. W. Bonfils (of the Denver Post family). Challenger Airlines flew from Salt Lake City to Denver via five Wyoming towns. Courtesy of Frontier Airlines.

Arizona Airways began in 1946 and flew intrastate routes radiating from Phoenix. Courtesy of Frontier Airlines.

# Bibliography

## Articles

"A New Anchorage for Eagles." *Architecture/Construction Symposia.* Vol. 1, No. 4, Sept. 1966, pp. 18–21.

Albright, Sydbet H, "The Fred Kelly Story." *American Aviation Historical Journal.* Vol. 13, No. 3 and 4, 1968.

"Death Over San Diego." *Time.* 9 Oct., 1978, pp. 16–20.

Pearson, John F. "Don't Sell the Airship Short." *Popular Mechanics.* Sept. 1974, pp. 112-117, 160.

Schefter, Jim. "New Aerodynamic Design, New Engines, Spawn a Revival of the SST." *Popular Science.* July 1979, pp. 62–65, 129–130.

Sullivan, John. "Who's Minding the Airport?" *Denver Magazine*, March 1979, pp. 33–36, 53.

## Books

Athearn, Robert G. *Union Pacific Country.* Chicago: Rand McNally, 1971.

Dorsett, Lyle W. *The Queen City: A History of Denver.* Boulder: Pruett Publishing Co., 1977.

Hosokawa, Bill. *Thunder in the Rockies: The Incredible Denver Post.* New York: William Morrow & Co., 1976.

Jones, William C. and Kenton Forrest. *Denver: A Pictorial History.* Boulder: Pruett Publishing Co., 1974.

Kelly, George V. *The Old Gray Mayors of Denver.* Boulder: Pruett Publishing Co., 1976.

Lethan, J. *Historical and Descriptive Reviews of Denver, Her Leading Business Houses and Enterprising Men.* Denver: Range Press, 1893?

Mumey, Nolie. *Colorado Airmail.* Denver: Range Press, 1977.

Mumey, Nolie. *Evolution of Flight.* Kendrick-Bellamy Company, 1931.

Noel, Thomas J. *Denver: Rocky Mountain Gold.* Tulsa: Continental Heritage Press, 1980.

Perkin, Robert L. *The First Hundred Years: An Informal History of Denver and the Rocky Mountain News, 1895–1959.* New York: Doubleday & Co., 1959.

Rosen, Stephen. *Future Facts.* New York: Simon & Schuster, 1976.

Taylor, Frank J. *High Horizons.* New York: McGraw-Hill Book Co., 1964.

## Periodicals

*Sky Chefs People* (Sky Chefs Corporation).
*Sunliner News* (Continental Airlines).
*The Golden Jet* (Frontier Airlines).
*Western's World* (Western Airlines).

## Newspapers

*Denver Post.*
*Denver Republican.*
*Rocky Mountain News.*

## Studies

Bureau of Business and Social Research (University of Denver), and Bureau of Business Research (University of Colorado). *Civil Aviation in the Denver Area Past and Prospective Growth.* Denver: Department of Improvements and Parks, City and County of Denver, 1948.

# Index

Numerals in italics indicate an illustration of the subject mentioned.